VOICES
FROM
OTHER
LIVES

VOICES FROM OTHER LIVES

Reincarnation as a Source of Healing

by Thorwald Dethlefsen
translated by Gerhard Hundt

M. EVANS AND COMPANY, INC.
New York, New York 10017

M. Evans and Company titles are distributed in
the United States by the J. B. Lippincott Company,
East Washington Square, Philadelphia, Pa. 19105;
and in Canada by McClelland & Stewart Ltd.,
25 Hollinger Road, Toronto M4B 3G2, Ontario

LIBRARY OF CONGRESS CATALOGING IN PUBLICATION DATA

Dethlefsen, Thorwald.
Voices from other lives: Reincarnation as a
source of healing.

Translation of Das Erlebnis der Wiedergeburt.
Includes bibliographical references.
1. Reincarnation. 2. Mental healing. I. Title.
BL515.D4513   133.9'013   76-30454
ISBN 0-87131-233-6

Design by Joel Schick

Manufactured in the United States of America

9 8 7 6 5 4 3 2 1

Although all personal information concerning research subjects and patients has been changed sufficiently to make identification impossible, distortion of contents has been carefully avoided. All printed records are available in the form of original taped segments in the archives of the Institute for Extraordinary Psychology in Munich.

Contents

*This book is dedicated
to all my patients and research subjects
who made this work possible.*

Instead of a Preface . . .

A few thoughts on the use of this book. You have bought this book (or perhaps only borrowed it . . .) and are now starting to read it. In the following pages, we discuss matters that are by no means considered obvious in our concept of world philosophy.

There are two ways to read a book: Either you will find your prior views and opinions confirmed, in which case you will certainly like this book.

Or you will discover with increasing displeasure that everything you find printed herein completely contradicts your prior beliefs. You will be indignant at our imputations and opinions.

If you belong to either of these groups, the book will have no value for you, because after reading it you will not have changed your attitude. For this reason, please try a third method of reading it. Put aside all preconceived notions and opinions for the duration of the book.

Try to understand it the way it is intended.

After completing it, survey it in its entirety and only then bring forth the old opinions and make comparisons.

Books should provide incentives for development. Fixation burdens all development.

Views that one is not prepared to change are fixations.

Our subject requires "flexible" readers. You will see why . . .

VOICES FROM OTHER LIVES

The
Experiment

*The theory of reincarnation
is a turning point
in the history of man.*
NIETZSCHE

THE BEGINNING

IT WAS ALMOST exactly seven years ago, in June 1968, that I first carried out the experiment that was to become the basis and starting point not only for my later research work, but also for my theory of life. I had no inkling of all this when I demonstrated a few experiments in hypnosis to a group of interested laymen. After my medium (a commonly used but somewhat unfortunate designation for the hypnotized person) had relived his past through me and had recalled a few incidents from his childhood, I tried to determine whether it might also be possible to remember one's own birth or perhaps even relive it. The attempt succeeded.

My medium, an engineer about twenty-five years of age, suddenly began, amid moaning and a changed breathing pattern, to describe his birth. This success, which surprised me, encouraged me to go back even further in time. I suggested to him that he was in his mother's womb, three months before birth, and he began to describe his impressions as an embryo! But this evening I wanted to know still more. I suggested, "Let us go back still further—until you come upon an event that you can picture and describe accurately. Go back that far in time!"

A tense pause ensued. My medium breathed heavily and finally began to speak in a choked voice. He told of his observations, and when I questioned him further, the interview crystallized into the story of a man whose name was Guy Lafarge, who was born in 1852, lived in Alsace, sold vegetables, and finally died in 1880 as a stable hand.

I then led my medium back into "this" life and awakened him. My subject, after this session, could only recall sleeping soundly and had forgotten everything else. This phenomenon of loss of memory after a deep hypnotic sleep is known as amnesia; it can appear by itself or can be induced through posthypnotic suggestion.

This experiment in age regression beyond birth to an existence that can be phenomenalistically described as a "former life" was repeated by me several times in the following weeks, sometimes with the same medium, sometimes with other subjects. The same results were obtained on each occasion. Whenever I led the subjects back through time, recollections of an existence would evolve that were in no way identical with that of the present. These recollections were so vivid that they appeared, not as something in the distant past, but as clear as something happening in the present.

It is not necessary to go into detail with regard to these experiments, since the records of these sessions have appeared word for word and were commented on in my book *The Life After Life*, published by Bertelsmann Publishers, Inc., Munich.

If only two years later I have written another book on the same subject, the reason can only be that by continuing these experiments at this time, we have expanded and developed not only the technique but also the knowledge that has been obtained, and both merit new consideration.

With my first experiments, I still had the feeling that I had achieved something truly rare, something sensational; a mixture of awe and fear frequently prevented me from carrying out the experiment. Only with subjects who were in deep hypnotic sleep did I dare to take the step beyond birth—but always coupled with a little fear, fear of the new and the unknown. I was also afraid every time I touched upon certain phases of the experiment, such as illnesses, accidents, or death. Every time I came across such a traumatic event, I quickly made a huge detour around it and immediately guided my subject back to "this" life. After every session, I breathed a sigh of relief that all had gone well and that my medium smiled cheerfully without knowing what he had experienced and talked about during the session.

In the meantime, much, yes almost everything, has changed completely. Fear has been replaced by experience, uncertainty by detailed knowledge of procedures. What years ago was an event for me is now my daily work. Where formerly I looked for only deep-sleep subjects, today regression to a "former life" succeeds with almost everyone, even when only moderate relaxation has been induced. This was accomplished by means of constant improvement in my regression technique, which today has become so finely tuned that I can find an "entrance" into almost every human being.

But the two most essential changes are the following:

1. My interest is to aim particularly at traumatic recollections; experiences such as accidents, illnesses, tortures, and death are relived with special intensity in every detail and

2. The contents of the entire session are now connected to conscious knowledge; the subject not only knows the contents of the session exactly, but can recall all former experiences with the same accuracy with which one remembers the previous day.

The result of this development is that the original experiment, "sensational" for many and "questionable" for many others, today has become a psychotherapeutic method that because of its success has impressed even its opponents with the philosophical consequences of the experiments. For we live in a world in which only the experiment and success count—both will be described in detail in the following pages.

THE EXPERIMENT TODAY

For all experiments, we selected almost exclusively subjects who had not been informed in advance of the nature and purpose of the undertaking and therefore entered the experiment "blindly." For this reason, newspaper advertisements with the following text were submitted by "neutral" individuals:

> CAN YOU BE HYPNOTIZED? ARE YOU INTERESTED IN YOUR SUBCONSCIOUS? WE ARE LOOKING FOR YOUNG PEOPLE (18–27) WITH HIGHER EDUCATION TO PARTICIPATE IN A SERIES OF TESTS.

On the average, between thirty and fifty interested persons responded to such notices and were invited to group meetings. In such a meeting, I would select those most suited for hypnosis by means of simple methods (pendulum test or waking suggestion). These individuals were then invited to a second group session in which I would again select the participants who reacted best. All these sessions were observed by outside witnesses, were recorded, and sometimes were also filmed. Those who survived this "double sorting-out process" would be invited to an individual session in which I carried out the regression.

For control purposes, witnesses would again be present and, in addition, all sessions were recorded on tape and many were filmed. At times, after each of the first two or three sessions, I would erase posthypnotically the subject's recollection of the contents of the session in order to be able to determine whether through repetition at varying time intervals the same information concerning a prior life would be forthcoming or whether the statements simply represented a spontaneous reaction. Only after several such repetitions did I make known the contents of the entire session by suggesting that after the session the subject could recall all details while awake. Up to this time, not a word was said about the purpose of the experiment; no mention was made of reincarnation, prior life, recollections, and so on. This procedure avoids the possibility of preparing the medium to expect situations that would cause his utterances during the session. This also weakens the possible accusation that I was using only persons predisposed to the occult, who believed in reincarnation from the start and who would therefore bring wishes, ideas, and flights of fancy in that direction to the session. Since the selection of subjects and the recording of interviews were conducted uninterruptedly by outside witnesses, it would not have been possible for me to prepare or influence subjects in advance.

The experiment itself was basically divided into three parts:

1. Inducement of hypnotic sleep.

2. Step-by-step regression of the subject along the time axis: reliving his birth—reliving his embryo condition—further regression until new impressions appear—drawing out the "prior life" in interview form.

3. Return to the present and awakening from the hypnosis.

During the experiment, the subject usually lies on a special relaxing couch and I sit next to him, while the recording personnel and the audience form a semicircle in front of us. In order to present a representative sampling of what actually occurs, the report of an actual session follows.

My subject in this case is a journalist who, as the result of my publications,* came to ask me whether I could perform this experiment on her. Of course, I hear this request frequently; in fact, it is usually imposed as a condition—"I will believe you only

---

* In the case of journalists and patients who have heard of or read about my experiments, one can naturally not rule out the factor of "expectation conditioning." I nevertheless believe that on the basis of my first "blind" attempts with subjects who had no indication of the purpose of my experiments, I have proved that there is no connection between expectation and result.

if you will try it on me." While, naturally, personal experience is the best way to convince someone, it nevertheless appears to me that this is expensive missionary work, in view of the numerical size of the human race. Nevertheless, I frequently yielded to people's requests to be allowed to participate as a subject.

After our first trial session, the journalist expressed grave doubts about the success of our venture because she did not believe she had been hypnotized deeply enough. This misunderstanding arises frequently, since the layman usually equates hypnosis with unconsciousness. When unconsciousness does not occur, he believes hypnosis does not work on him. I had considerably more confidence and invited her to a second session, during which I was already able to carry out the regression. Let it be noted here that there is not only a "prior life," but that one can constantly go back further in time. The theory will follow later. Here is the record:

(S = Subject; H = Hypnotist)

First Session

S: Medicinal—doesn't smell good—they say Mrs. Lurd is here —Mrs. Lurd—I don't know exactly what that means—they always say midwife and then they say I now have a little brother—hm, yes—look at him, hm, now I will certainly—oh, no—that's not a brother—that's a sister—now I'll have to push her around in the baby carriage again——I don't like to do that—I'm in the garden and the baby carriage is much bigger than I am.

H: How old are you?

S: Seven.

H: And what is your name?

S: They say Lenchen—I don't like myself.

H: Why not?

S: I am so ugly.

H: Did someone tell you that or did you decide that yourself?

S: Nah, they always say that.

H: Who?

S: My mother, my father, they say I'm terribly untidy—and I always wear black stockings—I don't like them either—but then I'll go to my aunt next door—she is also terribly untidy they say —but she gives me piano lessons, and then she is angry when I wipe the dust from the piano—I always draw pictures on the piano cover—my aunt is an old maid, and I'm really not supposed to visit her so often—my brother once fell into a tub with dirty clothes and they were angry—my aunt is a teacher—because she couldn't get a husband—they say—my aunt gives private lessons —the children learn French.

H: We shall leave these events. Let us go further back in time, because time means nothing to us. You are getting younger. You are now six years old—five—four. You are four years old. How do you feel?

S: I don't know—everything is so restless—my father is there, a man is there—that's my father—he scolded my mother because she gave someone sugar at the front door, and she said she was going to bring something—no, I don't know what—or she promised to bring sugar, if my mother gives her something, but she did not come back, and I am standing at the window and my mother is going to the station with my father. She is wearing a very long dress—my father is wearing a helmet with a point on top, and now they are going around the corner—yes.

H: Now let us go back further in your life, and let us agree, it doesn't matter how far back we go. You will always understand what I am saying. You are being born!

S: I don't know—that—I don't like that—no, it has a strange smell—they are hitting me—I don't want to—I don't want to— no—

H: What do you feel?

S: It is terrible—so wet and cold—

H: Do you see anything?

S: Yes, there are people.

H: Do you hear anything?

S: I don't want to—

H: Let us erase this impression—and go back a little further—let us go back about three months—it is three months before your birth—how do you feel now?

S: Good—it is warm—and beating.

H: What is your name?

S: I think my name is Ellen—but I don't know.

H: Let us leave this scene and go back further in time—not only months, but perhaps years—you yourself can decide how far—we will go back so far in time until we reach some new situation or a new event which you can describe in words . . .

S: There is some sort of house—near the convent—they don't want me there.

H: Who doesn't want you?

S: The people—because I'm going to have a baby—

H: So you know the people?

S: I must know them—but I don't want to know them—no, I don't want to be there.

H: How old are you?

S: Sixteen.

H: What is your name?

S: Anna.

H: And what else?

S: Oh, yes, I am at home—it's a very small village, it's beautiful there.

H: What is the name of the village?

S: Neuenbrook.

H: Where is that?

S: In the marsh—Dekling is up on the mountain and down there . . .

H: That's where you live?

S: Yes.

H: With your parents?

S: Yes.

H: What is your name?

S: Anna.

H: What else?

S: Schwenzer.

H: Can you spell that for me?

S: Hm, of course I can—my father would be angry—he is a teacher.

H: Here in the village?

S: Yes.

H: What is your father's name?

S: Johann.

H: And your mother's?

S: Anna.

H: And your name is Anna, too?

S: Hm.

H: What would you like to be some day?

S: A teacher.

H: And how old are you now?

S: Hmmm—fourteen.

H: And when is your birthday?

S: Sometime in spring.

H: Don't you know the exact date?

S: Yes—April 17th.

H: In what year were you born?

S: 1832—but we don't talk about that.

H: Why not?

S: That's not important. I am dreaming.

H: About whom?

S: I am dreaming that I am playing the organ—beautifully—composing beautiful poetry—I am somewhere where the whole world is beautiful.

H: Isn't it beautiful where you are?

S: Yes, but so cold—gray—and anyway—they say—I am—they say I'm a little crazy.

H: Who says that?

S: Oh, the people in the village—but my father doesn't say that.

H: And your mother?

S: She always has so much to do.

H: Why do people say you are crazy?

S: Don't know—because I'm not like them—I read and dream —and I . . .

H: What do you read?

S: History—exploration.

H: Do you have books?

S: Yes.

H: Can you name me one of your favorite books?

S: Yes, Tut—they say Tutan—he was a Pharaoh.

H: What is the name of the book?

S: I think they mispronounce it, Tutankhamen—I would have liked to live then.

H: What is in the book? What's it about?

S: About Egypt—how they lived—they already knew about beehive cakes—how to bake them—my father took me along to church—I was allowed to play the organ—but the pedals are so far down— I would like to sit in this church and be able to play everything.

H: Now tell me what is important to you.

S: How the farmers feel—what the weather is like—how the cows—I must learn to milk them.

H: Do you have your own cows?

S: Yes, I think so—two.

H: Do you own a farm?

S: No, but a little house—with very small windows—a bull's-eye glass.

H: What is your favorite food?

S: Fruit pudding.

H: What?

S: Fruit pudding with milk.

H: What is that made of?

S: I don't know—we always have it. The main street is always terribly muddy on my birthday.

H: Why?

S: It rains so much—but my father—he always plays the organ in church—I like to go there—I would like to do that some day.

H: Do you have brothers or sisters?

S: Yes.

H: How many?

S: I don't know—suddenly I can't see them—two brothers, I think.

H: What are their names?

S: Hans—Gottlob.

H: Are they older or younger than you?

S: I don't know. I am always alone.

H: Why?

S: Because I like to be alone.

H: What do you do—when you are alone?

S: ——

H: Let us go a little further along in your life—you are a year older—you will be fifteen years old—what happened to your parents, what happened in the village during the past year?

S: I am out of school—too bad.

H: And what are you doing now?

S: They say I must go to work—would very much like to learn something, but we have no money—and so they brought me to this house—it's so cold.

H: Where is this house?

S: In Itzehoe.

H: Where?

S: In Itzehoe.

H: What kind of house is it?

S: It is sort of light gray and has one story—it's near the convent—but I don't want to go there!

H: Is the house part of the convent?

S: No.

H: A private house?

S: Yes.

H: Who lives in it?

S: A doctor—but they're not good to me.

H: Why not?

S: I do nothing but clean.

H: Is this where you work?

S: Yes.

H: What is the doctor's name?

S: [*The name was given but has been stricken from the record.*]

H: And all you do there is clean?

S: Yes, I don't do it very well—it's so monotonous.

H: Do you ever get time to read?

S: No.

H: What do you do when you have free time?

S: I go into the woods, run around—hear music—hm, not a soul is there.

H: What year is this?

S: 1848.

H: How old are you?

S: Sixteen.

H: Let us go a year further in your life—you are a year older—tell me whether anything has changed since last year—what is new in your life? Where are you and what are you doing?

S: I am no longer there.

H: Then what are you doing?

S: I am not doing well.

H: Why not?

S: I don't know where to go.

H: Why don't you know?

S: I'm still looking.

H: For a job?

S: No, some place to go—there is something—there is some sort of home.

H: Can't you go to your parents?

S: I don't want them to know'

H: Know what?

S: Hm—I'm going to have a baby!

H: Why didn't you stay in your job?

S: They don't want me anymore.

H: And where do you sleep now?

S: Outside.

H: Who is the father of your child?

S: I am not allowed to say.

H: Why not?

S: He said I am not allowed to tell—I don't want to.

H: What don't you want?

S: Hm [*deep sigh*]— I'm going to a sanctuary.

H: And then what will you do?

S: I am going there.

H: What year is this?

S: 1849.

H: What month is it?

S: May, I believe—May 14.

H: How many months are you along?

S: I don't know that.

H: Today is May 14. What are you doing?

S: I'm going to the sanctuary.

H: At what time?

S: Five o'clock.

H: In the evening or morning?

S: In the morning.

H: And then?

S: Then I am going in.

H: What do you feel?

S: Peace.

H: You are not afraid?

S: No, I only want peace.

H: Are you finding it?

S: Yes.

H: How do you feel now?

S: Fine—free.

H: Where are you?

S: At home.

H: Where?

S: Where I have always lived, but they don't see me.

H: What can you see?

S: Everything—my mother is constantly saying, "What a

shame, what a shame."

H: But they don't see you?

S: No.

H: What do you experience when you see and hear your mother?

S: Hm, I'm somewhat sad.

H: And what is your father saying?

S: Nothing—he is sad.

H: They know of your death?

S: I didn't die!

H: Then what are you?

S: I am alive!

H: Then why don't they see you?

S: I don't want to be there anymore. I want to sleep.

H: Where are you going now?

S: No place—I'm still in the village—but then I'm not there anymore.

H: What is your name now?

S: Hm—nothing.

H: What are you doing there? Whom do you particularly like to visit?

S: Just looking—I see everything.

H: Do you feel especially well in this condition?

S: Yes.

H: Is it pleasant?

S: Yes.

H: What else is going on?

S: Nothing.

H: Will you be born again?

S: I don't know that.

H: Would you like to?

S: No—oh—oh, I believe I will have to be born again, but I don't want to—oh—I feel something like that.

H: Do you believe there is a reason for it?

S: Perhaps I am being punished.

H: What for?

S: But all I wanted was peace—I don't want to be born again.

H: Where are you now?

S: I have a mother again!

H: Did you pick her out?

S: No.

H: Did you feel it, when you were being born?

S: No.

H: But you have a mother again?

S: Yes.

H: Are you with her now?

S: Yes.

H: How big are you?

S: Ho—ho—very small. How big? I don't know.

H: Do you like your mother?

S: I don't know her yet.

H: Can you connect her with anything?

S: She looks like—she looks familiar to me.

H: Whom does she resemble?

S: I've seen her face before.

H: You will now remember when and where. Tell me!

S: Yes, in a village where I once lived—

H: Who was she then?

S: She was already my mother then.

H: She was already your mother at that time?

S: Yes.

H: Are you positive?

S: I don't want to!

H: How old are you now?

S: I don't know yet.

H: Let us return to the moment of your birth. You are just being born.

S: Yes.

H: You are being born again—do you still know your mother?

S: Yes.

H: From where?

S: She looks so familiar to me.

H: Do you like her?

S: I don't even know her.

H: But she looks familiar to you?

S: Yes.

H: How do you feel toward her?

S: She is good to me—they seem to be glad that I'm here.

H: Are you glad, too?

S: No—now everything is starting all over again.

H: Do you know what will happen to you?

S: Yes.

H: What will happen?

S: I will be terribly alone.

H: Just as it was once before?

S: Yes—even worse. I must get away from there—then . . .

H: From where?

S: From there.

H: Where is there?

S: There is—there are gravestones—and there is a cemetery, and my father is making gravestones—and they don't like me. Sometimes a funeral procession passes the house and goes up the hill to the grave—to the cemetery—then I stand on top of a gravestone, and I think they will buy me—then I can get away—

H: Let us return to the time of your birth. Tell me the date of your birth.

S: September.

H: September what?

S: The sixth.

H: What time?

S: In the morning.

H: Tell me the exact time.

S: Twenty minutes before nine.

H: You are getting older and bigger. We shall take large strides forward in your life, with no delay.

Second Session

S: I am afraid—I must get dressed, and then we are all sitting near the front door—my brother—my mother and a girl, it is thundering—I'm terribly afraid.

H: How old are you?

S: I don't know exactly—perhaps three, four; I am still very small but I can already dress myself—then we go up the stairs again, my mother gets a ladder, and we go, we climb up the ladder, up to the attic, and we look out and we can see the marsh where there's a fire, where the lightning struck—my mother loves to see that—whenever there's a fire, she runs out of the house and has to go where the fire is—actually I do, too—but I'm not allowed, and I don't like thunderstorms—I'm always afraid—

H: Let us leave this experience and go back further in time —because time means nothing to us; time is nothing more than a sign of agreement, a measure that does not exist in reality. We shall go back in time, and the past becomes the present. You are getting younger and ever smaller—getting to be two years old— we are going back further—you are a year old—how are you?

S: I am lying in a laundry basket and hm—don't know why —it is actually—oh—they are moving out—

H: Who are they?

S: Well, my mother, my father, I think there's a girl there, too—a servant girl—yes, we're moving out of the first floor and into a house—I will grow up in this house—but the reason I'm in the laundry basket—they are packing.

H: We shall leave this experience and go back further, because time means nothing to us. We shall go back to the moment of your birth. You are just being born. What do you feel?

S: I don't want to.

H: Why not?

S: No, I don't want to, I don't want to be born!

H: Do you have a reason?

S: I am afraid.

H: Of what?

S: I want it to be peaceful and quiet, as it was.

H: Were you on earth before?

S: Yes.

H: Was that long ago?

S: I don't know.

H: Can you recall it?

S: Yes, I was quite a poor girl—I had smooth pigtails and I was not pretty, I always wore wooden slippers, they were always dirty, that was—there were so many meadows.

H: Let us go back so far in time until we reach the exact moment you are talking about. We shall go back in time until we reach the exact moment you are talking about and you will recall—everything will be the present and you will tell me about yourself! What is your name?

S: Anna.

H: What else?

S: The rest of my name? I'm more than a meter tall.

H: And how old are you?

S: I must be about ten.

H: Then you must know your name.

S: Of course—Schwenzer—yes, Anna Schwenzer.

H: What year is this?

S: 18—I read that somewhere—yes, 1842.

H: When were you born?

S: 1832.

H: The date?

S: April—in April.

H: April what?

S: Thirteen, fourteen, fifteen, sixteen, seventeen . . . I believe the seventeenth, yes!

H: Do you have sisters or brothers?

S: I don't think so—I am still to get some—but yes, I think—I have two brothers.

H: And what else will you be getting?

S: A sister.

H: Let us move forward a bit—until you have a sister—how old are you now?

S: I don't know her at all. I am already gone.

H: What is your sister's name?

S: Helma.

H: What year was she born?

S: I must know her—I think it was about 1843—no—44 . . .

H: Do you know her now or not?

S: Yes.

H: Do you like your sister?

S: She is so small and very sweet.

H: What is your father's name?

S: My father's name is Hans—Johann—they call him Hans.

H: What does your father do?

S: He is a teacher—teacher and organist—that's nice.

H: And what do you like to do? Do you like to go to school?

S: Yes, very much.

H: Do you like to read books, too?

S: I read—I play the piano.

H: What do you play?

S: Oh—"The Happy Farmer"—I can't play it well, but it's a pretty melody.

H: Can you hum it for me?

S: (*Hums*) Oh, I can't sing.

H: And what do you like to read?

S: Hm, well, all—there is so much that interests me—travel, exploration—when I grow up, I shall travel all over the world!

H: Where, for example?

S: To the Holy Land.

H: Have you read about it?

S: In the Bible.

H: What else do you like to read?

S: Igot Igwadran—I think—I don't know for sure.

H: What else, what can you recall, books that you especially like?

S: Travel books and *Moses in Egypt.*

H: Do you have the book *Moses in Egypt*?

S: No, they build the pyramids there, it's described in the book, yes, that might be *Moses in Egypt*—and the wandering of the children of Israel through the wilderness—I'm particularly interested in that.

H: Can you describe for me one of the rooms in which you

live? Do you have a living room, or where do you like to spend your time?

S: Yes, we sit in the kitchen most of the time.

H: What does the kitchen look like?

S: There's a stove in the middle—there's always fire in it—and my mother has a very long apron with flounces—and the pots are all black.

H: Do you have a dishwashing machine?

S: What?

H: Don't you have anything like that?

S: We wash the dishes and we get water from the pump.

H: Where is the pump?

S: Outside in the yard.

H: Do you have a living room or a parlor?

S: We have a very small, very small parlor.

H: Can you tell me what it looks like?

S: There is a corner bench, and a niche where my mother keeps flowers, but she says fuchsia bring bad luck, so she puts them out, but I took them up in the attic with me—that's where I sleep—I'm not afraid of bad luck—but in winter it's very cold up there—I get cold easily—I'd like to go back to some place where it's warm.

H: Have you ever been where it's very warm?

S: Yes.

H: When was that? Where was that? Was that in this life?

S: No.

H: Good, let's go back a bit further—let's go back to the time of your birth. You are getting younger, smaller—you are just being born—and we shall not remain here. We shall go back further—past your birth and even further, until you are in an entirely new situation. What do you see?

S: It is hot—it's the desert.

H: What are you doing in the desert?

S: I—I have sheep. I am walking around with the sheep.

H: Are you herding them?

S: Yes, but there is so much room.

H: What is your name?

S: Ruth.

H: And what else?

S: I don't know.

H: Your name is only Ruth?

S: Yes.

H: What year is this?

S: I don't know.

H: Can you tell me approximately?

S: 100.

H: In what country are you?

S: In the Holy Land.

H: Why is this land holy?

S: Because God speaks to us.

H: Who is "us"? What is "our" name? What do you call yourselves?

S: We are a tribe.

H: What is the name of your tribe?

S: We are the Maccabees.

H: Tell me about this tribe.

S: We have tents—my father is a very powerful man.

H: What is his name?

S: Hohas.

H: Again.

S: Hohas, I think.

H: You are now standing before your father. You will tell him something—and in the language that you normally speak.

S: Honaihn—I am really not supposed to speak to him.

H: Why not?

S: One must wait until he speaks.

H: What did he just say to you?

S: Hot maihn—master.

H: And what are you saying now?

S: I am getting water, a great deal—I have to go a long way —to find water.

H: Where are you getting the water?

S: I don't know—I walk and walk and don't find any—then suddenly I come upon a mountain.

H: Do you know the name of the mountain?

S: It has no name—but I find water there—

H: Where?

S: It comes out of the mountain—my lips are all dry and I'm tired—but one is not allowed to say that.

H: But you are allowed to drink the water now?

S: No.

H: Why not?

S: . . . It belongs to my father.

H: How do you say water in your language?

S: I don't know—brut—flepp.

H: How do you feel?

S: Tired.

H: What makes you tired?

S: Walking and walking—and stones and stones.

H: How are you dressed?

S: I'm wearing something very coarse—sandals and a coarse robe.

H: How do you look?

S: Black hair—black—I don't know exactly how I look—I know I am thin—but I don't know how I look.

H: Do you know Christ? Have you heard of Him?

S: No—but it is said a Messiah is coming.

H: When will He come?

S: Everyone is waiting—He is to save us—but by that time we shall all be dead.

H: How old will you get to be?

S: Hm, twenty-five.

H: Good, let us go forward to your twenty-fifth year. How do you feel?

S: Tired.

H: Tired? Tired from what?

S: We walk and walk, I can't make it anymore.

H: Why? Are you sick?

S: We have no water. The others are continuing.

H: And you?

S: I am staying—it's fine here.

H: Where are you staying?

S: I will simply remain lying on the ground.

H: And what happens then?

S: It is getting dark—it is getting very quiet—I am falling asleep.

H: And what happens now—what comes next?

S: I see myself lying there.

H: What are you doing?

S: I need not walk anymore. I no longer need to look for water.

H: Can you tell me the year in which this is happening? This change from existence to nonexistence?

S: About 100.

H: Good—tell me more about what is happening—you need not walk anymore, you need not get water anymore—where are you?

S: I have caught up with the others.

H: How?

S: Very simply. But no one speaks of me anymore—they are sitting down—they have built a fire—and one of my father's wives says she is not going any further either—she is also tired —I tell her to close her eyes—fall asleep—come with me—it is very nice.

H: Does she believe you?

S: Not right away—and then I lose her!

H: And how are you getting along now? What are you doing?

S: I can find no one—no one.

H: You are all alone?

S: Yes.

H: Do you like that?

S: Yes.

H: What will happen to you now? Will you stay here always—in this way?

S: No.

H: No? What will change? How will you continue?

S: This is strange—I am—I will be—somewhere else.

H: Where?

S: In a castle.

H: When will that be? Soon?

S: That is—in Bohemia.

H: Let us go back to this point in time—

S: I have a husband—he is very domineering.

H: What is his name?

S: Eckehard.

H: What is your name?

S: . . . Ursula.

H: What year is this?

S: 1580.

H: And you live in Bohemia? How are you getting along?

S: I cannot stand that man.

H: Why not?

S: He is mean—mean.

H: What did he do to you?

S: He beats, he beats the people, and he beats me, too.

H: What does your husband do? What is his occupation?

S: Nothing, he is a lord.

H: What is his name? Does he have a title?

S: He is a baron. No, he has followers—he is an officer—no, it's not called officer—he is a knight—and he has soldiers.

H: What is the name of the place where you live—is it a city?

S: No.

H: Then what?

S: It is a castle.

H: What is the name of the castle?

S: Strachwitz—I am not sure.

H: Why not? Of course, you know that!

S: Strachwitz, but I think, it doesn't seem right—I'm searching —I'm searching.

H: Tell me something else. How old are you?

S: Twenty-three.

H: When were you married?

S: Two years ago.

H: What was your maiden name?

S: I can't think of the name!

H: What is your name now?

S: Strachwitz.

H: Your husband's name?

S: Yes.

H: Was the castle named after him?

S: I don't know—they have lived there a long time.

H: Tell me, where is this castle located?

S: There is a river.

H: What is the name of the river?

S: That is the Moldau.

H: What else is near the castle?

S: Mountains.

H: Is there a big city nearby?

S: Prague.

H: Have you ever been in Prague?

S: Yes—we went with the carriage—six hours.

H: How do you like Prague?

S: It was very nice—I stood on a bridge there—no—no—it wasn't nice, it wasn't nice at all.

H: Why not, what happened?

S: I saw many corpses in the water.

H: What is the name of your ruler?

S: There is a king.

H: And what is the name of the king?

S: Alfred, I think—but I—strange—I have trouble remembering.

H: Very well, let's go on a little further in your life—you are getting older—will you have children?

S: No.

H: Are you still with your husband?

S: Yes, he took me along.

H: Where to?

S: We're no longer in the castle.

H: Then where are you?

S: In Nuremberg.

H: How old are you now?

S: Thirty-six.

H: Thirty-six, and you are living in Nuremberg with your husband now?

S: Yes.

H: Where? In a house or in a castle?

S: In a house—but there is a castle—a fortress, I think, nearby.

H: And you are living there? Why aren't you there anymore now?

S: There is a war.

H: Who against whom?

S: There is war everywhere.

H: What sort of war is it? Why are they fighting?

S: The Bohemians, the Swedes.

H: What is your husband doing in the war?

S: He is roaming around—and he brought me to his aunt.

H: To Nuremberg?

S: Yes.

H: What is the name of this aunt?

S: Hatteline von Strachwitz.

H: And she lives in Nuremberg?

S: Yes.

H: What year is this?

S: 1623.

H: We shall go forward in your life—until there is a change again.

S: Fire.

H: What is it?

S: Fire—it is burning—all the houses are burning.

H: Where?

S: In Nuremberg—I can't get any air—I can't get air—hm [*moans and writhes*].

H: Go forward—let us leave this incident—let us go forward just a bit—look back and tell us what happened.

S: Hm, I don't know.

H: Yes, you know.

S: It felt like cotton on my face—and I couldn't breathe and . . .

H: You are very calm.

S: No, that was the fire—I don't know where I am.

H: Can you tell me in what year you had that experience?

S: 16—I think—I don't know exactly—about 1630.

H: Yes, and in the mean time you have freed yourself from that experience and are now in a different situation—how do you like it now?

S: Fine.

H: What are you doing here?

S: Nothing.

H: How will it continue?

S: Very well, I am relieved.

H: Will you stay here always, in your relieved condition?

S: At first, yes.

H: And then?

S: I will float away.

H: Where to?

S: I will float away to the north—it is cold there—

H: Have you been born?

S: Soon, I think . . .

H: Good, let us proceed to the moment of your birth. Tell me the date you were born.

S: 1832.

H: Tell me the exact date.

S: Thirteen, fourteen, fifteen, sixteen, seventeenth of April.

H: April 17? Why do you start with the thirteenth?

S: That's when it started!

H: What started?

S: My mother wanted me born then.

H: And she wasn't able to?

S: It didn't happen that fast.

H: Why?

S: It didn't work, they got a woman from the city—she had to help.

H: And on the seventeenth it happened?

S: Yes.

H: Tell me the exact time.

S: Half-past eight.

H: In the morning?

S: Yes.

H: In what town were you born?

S: Neuenbrook.

H: Did the birth proceed smoothly?

S: No.

H: What happened during the birth?

S: They pulled on me terribly—I came into the world feet first—then they were afraid for me—but then all went well.

H: Look at your mother.

S: She has a small face.

H: Have you ever before, at any time in the past, seen this person?

S: Yes—I think so.

H: When and where?

S: That was far away.

H: Where—can you remember?

S: She lived in the sand.

H: What was your relationship to her at that time?

S: She was my sister.

H: Did you like her then?

S: My father liked her better.

H: Now she is your mother?

S: Yes.

H: Have you ever seen her since that time?

S: There was a time—I have difficulty remembering—I don't know.

H: Yes, you are getting older, older and taller, you are growing up—how old are you now?

S: Ten.

H: You are now twelve, fourteen . . .

S: Yes.

H: How do you feel?

S: I am sad.

H: Why?

S: I am no longer in school, and I wanted so much to learn.

H: What did you want to be?

S: Teacher, but there is no school for girls.

H: Very well, you are a year older, you will be fifteen—what are you doing now?

S: I am in the city.

H: What is the name of the city?

S: Itzehoe.

H: And where are you?

S: Behind the convent yard.

H: And what are you doing there?

S: I work there as a maid.

H: For whom are you working? What is your master's name?

S: Doctor—hm—yes, a little fat man (*she names him*).

H: And what is his first name?

S: (*She gives his name.*)

H: We shall proceed about a year further in your life. Has anything changed? Tell us something!

S: He was very mean.

H: Yes, who is "he"?

S: Yes, he is (*name as above*).

H: Why was he mean?

S: I told him that I was going to have a baby—

H: And what did he say?

S: He said, "You whore, that isn't mine!"

H: And is it his?

S: Yes, whose otherwise?

H: And who is this man?

S: He—his wife must not know—and I'm not permitted to tell anyone!

H: What will you do?

S: I don't know.

H: Let us move on in time—further forward—what are you doing now?

S: I have thought about it—all night—I am tired—I don't want to go on—I am cold—I don't want to go on—not a soul will help me.

H: What are you doing?

S: I am going—going to the sanctuary—to the dike—and it is still dark—if it were light, I couldn't do it.

H: What date is this?

S: September—it is cold.

H: September what?

S: I don't know exactly—the thirteenth, I think. And I don't know anyone I can ask.

H: What time is it?

S: It is five in the morning—I didn't sleep all night.

H: What are you doing now?

S: I will sit by the dike for a while.

H: And then?

S: There is no—there is no choice—you must—you must do it it is cold—I will close my eyes—soon, soon I will have peace.

H: What will happen now?

S: Hm. [*cries*]

H: Leave this situation. What happens now? Where are you now?

S: I am looking.

H: Where?

S: They have found me.

H: And what are they doing?

S: They are asking my father whether I was wearing a red dress. Look, my father is crying—hm, I don't like to see him cry. What was I to do? [*cries*]

H: What will happen to you now?

S: Next I am at home—

H: Let us continue.

S: My mother isn't crying at all—she is only angry.

H: Let us continue—what happens now?

S: Nothing.

H: Let us go forward in time again—until something changes.

S: Aha.

H: What is happening?

S: She took me along.

H: Who?

S: My mother.

H: Where to?

S: To herself.

H: What do you mean by that?

S: I don't want that.

H: What did she do?

S: I don't want it.

H: Tell me, where are you?

S: She is giving birth to me.

H: Good, tell me the year of your birth.

S: 1912.

H: Now you are born again!

S: They would have preferred a son—but I am here instead.

H: You are getting older and you are growing, correct?

S: Yes.

H: We shall go forward in time now, without delay, always forward—you are ten, fifteen, twenty years old, thirty-five, forty, forty-five. We shall go forward until we have reached the year 1975. We shall proceed to January 31, 1975, and there we shall stop—we shall stop on January 31, 1975—when you have reached this date, say so!

S: Yes.

H: You are in a deep, hypnotic sleep. You feel well, very well, happy and satisfied. You have completed a long journey, a journey with your soul and through your soul. You will slowly release yourself from all these incidents and experiences and completely immerse yourself in a feeling of rest and relaxation. You feel well and happy and contented. You are sleeping deeply and soundly, very deeply and very soundly—and in this absolute rest, your complete organism will regenerate itself. Your entire body will recuperate, create new strength—you are feeling well —very well, happy and satisfied—you feel well and content— sleep deeply and soundly.

After these two sessions, the journalist had some of her statements checked out. As a result, the historic existence of an Anna Schwenzer, born April 17, 1832, at Neuenbrook, was verified. We were further able to learn from currently living members of the Strachwitz family that their family tree can actually be traced back to the Bohemian period described, although data from this period are missing.

A language expert identified the few foreign words from the subject's third prior life as Aramaic.

Further verification is not available thus far.

The Experiment in Cross-Examination

*I am just as certain as you see me here that
I have existed a thousand times before and
I hope to return a thousand times more.*
GOETHE TO FALK

THUS FAR, I have always spoken of "the previous life," "recollections of a prior life," "reincarnation"—concepts that are far from self-evident in the existing world. The quotation marks in which these concepts were placed are supposed to represent their hypothetical, temporary nature, because only now that we have had a closer look at the phenomenological side of the experiment can we turn to a closer examination of it.

If one talks about or describes such an experiment to a person who has not previously had any contact with this area, one can in most cases expect at best either indignation or a sympathetic smile at such flights of imagination (or, more plainly stated, nonsense). People who have had an opportunity to experience these experiments as observers react with considerably less uncertainty, and the easiest to convince are the subjects themselves, because what an individual has experienced, he need not take on faith—he knows it.

It is not at all surprising that my claim that reincarnation exists and that I could experimentally learn about anyone's "prior life" and make him conscious of it would meet with strong opposition from the public. Anything new that deviates from the normal always meets with opposition. Every human being finds it necessary to incorporate new information into an available storage file. This file is nothing more than the sum total of all previously obtained knowledge, or the person's learning history. If one, for example, receives information that does not fit into this file, fear arises as an expression of the conflict between the desire to be able to insert all information and the obvious impossibility of being able to do so in a specific instance. In order to eliminate the threat of this fear, the individual tries to change and mold the information until it fits into his file; the change is always made with the new information, since it is inconceivable that one would question one's sum total of learning because of a new bit of information.

A simple example may illustrate the above. Imagine a person alone at night in a large house. Suddenly he hears a muffled sound. This sound is new information that, quick as lightning, arouses fear. The individual will immediately look for means of fitting the information, in this case the muffled sound, logically into the file. His consciousness will try to compare the sound with all previous experiences in order to insert it according to the law of similarity. In this case, all possibilities are considered, from thunder to an intruder, until finally the following hypothesis is reached: "The cat must have knocked the letter file off the desk again." In that same moment, the tension eases, fear subsides, and the information is inserted. Whether the accepted correlation between sound and incident corresponds to reality is now completely immaterial.

This mechanism serves the learning process of man, because without the principles of insertion, assimilation, comparison, and recognition, there would be no learning progress—with each bit of new information, one would have to start from the beginning, like a child. Unfortunately, this valuable mechanism is also the cause of prejudices, opinions, and hypotheses. For this reason, we should keep in mind this incident, which was resolved for the most part unconsciously and with lightning rapidity, when we try to observe our experiments objectively and without prejudice, without forcing them unquestioningly into existing files and clichés. After all, every invention, every development, and all progress can originate only when someone believes something is basically possible, even though it was previously outside our learning experience. If no one had ever had the courage to believe it possible for man to fly, there would be no airplanes today. While we accept it as obvious today, the first persons to dare to think about this were laughed at and considered mad.

Now, while the concept of reincarnation is by no means new, it does not fit into the thought file of today's materialistic-scientific world philosophy. Science claims that consciousness exists only in connection with matter. This, however, is an assertion or an axiom that can claim validity only until such time as the opposite has been proved. In order to prove the opposite, let us determine whether my experiments can be explained within the scope of traditional thought and determine also how much force will be required to squeeze the results of those experiments into the existing file.

In the meantime, I have demonstrated my experiments to many people; journalists, laymen, and scientists. I have asked them their opinions, talked about these opinions and debated them. The many objections, attempted explanations, and assumptions can finally be summed up in four hypotheses that must be taken seriously. This does not include the objections that dismiss everything as pure and deliberate fraud. I find it pointless to try to defend oneself seriously against accusations of deceit; may this claim remain as a last refuge for those who cannot tolerate any truth other than their own do-it-yourself reality.

Herewith the four categories in which one can look for possible explanations:

1. The suggestion hypothesis supposes the possibility that the particular circumstances of the hypnosis may make it possible for the hypnotist to suggest an answer to the subject. This hypothesis is probably the easiest to refute, because a careful reading of the records will show that almost every question is formulated briefly and tersely and that in connection therewith not the slightest effort is made to conceal the answer within the question. In fact, I regularly insert a number of knowingly suggestive catch questions in which I ask about types of automobiles, modern appliances such as television and telephone, or contemporary persons. In not a single instance did a subject ever respond to such a modern concept, even when I suggestively inserted, "Surely you own a television set!" On the contrary, the subject always asked, in surprise, what sort of word this was. In one session, during which I frequently inserted modern words, my subject reacted angrily and complained that I was always talking "silly nonsense." When during a suitable situation I mentioned a "carton of milk" my subject broke out into resounding laughter—a "carton of milk" was completely beyond her comprehension. All in all, there is no evidence that an answer could be coerced by the nature of questioning or by suggestive formulation.

2. The second hypothesis that one hears with surprising frequency is the supposition that I transmit the desired answers not by my choice of words, but by the use of telepathy. For the materialistic-scientifically oriented person, telepathy would not appear to be the most logical answer, because telepathy, in spite of efforts to prove it statistically, also has not yet found a place in his theory of life. Nevertheless, its existence is being accepted more and more in ever widening circles, with the result that many parapsychologists are engaged in reducing all other "paranormal phenomena" to telepathy.

While it may some day be fundamentally possible to develop telepathy to the point where it could serve as an adequate means of communication, today we are still happy if we can only succeed in transmitting a few pictures or geometric figures in this manner. Considering today's accomplishments in the field of telepathy, I always feel greatly honored when someone seriously believes that I can transmit entire novels to my subjects by this means. If I could do this, I would only transmit data that could easily, quickly, and safely be proved. (This point is also overlooked by all who suspect deliberate fraud!)

I can assure all those who may suspect that I can unknowingly transmit answers by telepathy that on many occasions when I expected certain answers, they turned out quite differently. And the suspicion that my subjects might tap me telepathically has little validity, since I am not very well educated when it comes to history.

Hypotheses that talk of "wandering clairvoyants" or of "reading the Akasha Chronicles" also miss their mark. In both instances, it is surmised that a person in a particular hypnotic condition is in a position to receive information that falls outside the realm of his personal experience and outside of time and place limitations. Although we know that such phenomena are possible, we do not know enough about the regularity of their occurrence to allow us to occupy ourselves with these concepts with any degree of certainty. For this reason, I shall first disregard them in our case because there is not much to be gained by explaining one unknown with another unknown. Later on, when I discuss the therapeutic effectiveness of my experiments, we shall see that the assumption that in these experiments we are dealing with personal material will appear more plausible than the hypotheses of the expansion of perceptiveness in collective areas.

3. The inheritance hypothesis is what I like to call the attempted explanation that denies reincarnation and therefore assumes that the events and experiences of ancestors are transferred to their descendants by a genetic code. According to this theory, it is believed that everything a person experiences, indeed everything that he sees and feels, is stored up inside him. In the creation of a child, not only the "learning experiences" of both parents but the learning histories of all ancestors are joined together and are passed on by means of the genetic code. With

every new birth, the information is raised to a higher power and nothing is lost. Every human being could therefore draw on a gigantic reservoir of historic information that goes back as far in time as the history of human development.

From a scientific point of view, we are still far from certain as to whether learning experiences can be inherited. Even if experiments with animals were to indicate that learning can be inherited, the inheritance hypothesis would be eliminated as an explanation for our experiments for the following reasons: In our experiments, we obtain descriptions of clearly defined lives and not a potpourri of all sorts of recollections. Each life shows marked characteristics of a very specific personality whose individual parts form one complete entity. Even when the inheritance theory is given credit for this accomplishment, these "lives" would have to coincide exclusively with those of a subject's ancestors—but this is hardly ever the case. Added to this is the fact that in such descriptions one would obviously have to find the incisive events of one's own parents' lives—this likewise has never occurred. The hypothesis fails totally when it comes to the after-death descriptions of my subjects. In connection with the next hypothesis, we shall discuss a number of details that also cannot be explained via the inheritance theory.

Finally, should all these objections not suffice as a refutation, one could undoubtedly achieve clarity with a twin experiment. Twins, which are already siblings, would have to possess the identical genetic remembrance code and therefore make identical statements. I have not had the opportunity to experiment with twins, but even without this experiment I consider this hypothesis completely untenable.

4. The last remaining and most frequently advanced hypothesis is the one that, to sum up, I like to call the fantasy hypothesis. For most people, this is undoubtedly the most obvious explanation, and it would appear to be difficult to refute. Behind the fantasy hypothesis is the assumption that reports concerning a "former life" are nothing more than a fantastic manipulation of data that were somehow injected into this life

and stored up at random intervals. It is believed that through hypnosis and the accompanying intensified recollection capability, stories from the past, history, novels, and the like can be converted to a new entity and be made to appear as something that one has personally experienced. The subject, however, is not accused of fraudulent intent because this happens subconsciously, motivated by the desire to oblige the hypnotist and accede to his requests.

If one speaks of fantasy, one must assume that it deals with the rearranging of stored-up information, because "pure fantasy" is impossible without the use of existing data. Even in fantasy, only known information can be elicited, never anything absolutely new. For example, in fantasy one might picture a pink elephant flying through the air. This vision is only possible because each of the elements of this picture is known to us from experience: the elephant, the pink color, and the act of flying. The fantasy is obtained only by virtue of the new combination. It is, however, impossible to visualize a "krakilbastus" in fantasy, simply because we do not possess the suitable learning experience. One should never forget, therefore, that in considering the concept of fantasy one must always deal with stored-up material.

In spite of everything, it will be necessary to clarify whether or not in our experiments we are dealing only with personally experienced events. The experience of the experimental daydream technique, today known by the name of "catathymic picture life" or "symbol drama," speaks for this assumption. In this psychotherapeutic technique, the patient, while in a hypnotic-like state, experiences situations that during the moment of experience may contain a high semblance of reality but nevertheless represent only the symbolic treatment of his life problems as in a night dream. In the field of psychoanalytical experience, such symbolic treatment of an intrinsic problem would be nothing new. Even the therapeutic effectiveness of such a "symbol drama" would be psychodynamically explainable.

For all these reasons, the most obvious explanation actually appears to be that reports of alleged prior lives are really nothing more than carefully treated individual bits of information that were injected into this life in various ways.

But when we survey a larger series of experiments with the most widely varied subjects, this hypothesis more than ever loses its plausibility. First of all is the manner in which the subject relives certain events—it is not merely a simple recollection, not just the telling or piecing together of various isolated facts, but the subject relives his "experiences" with his entire body and with all his emotions. Unfortunately, the intensity of this reliving cannot be reproduced in writing; one has to have experienced such a session personally to be able to determine whether the nature of the reproduction more closely resembles a fabrication or a bringing into the present of an earlier experience. Almost everyone who has ever had the opportunity to attend such a session in person will corroborate the impression formulated by Professor Rainer Fuchs as follows:

> The reproduction of the material clearly showed the outcome of recollection and the return to what had been experienced and undergone. Not only were situations recalled, but inclinations and disinclinations, likes and dislikes were reactivated as they related to given situations. In addition, the life history was accurate to an amazing degree and correctly situated within the historical-sociological framework.

This reliving is so intense that in some situations it seizes the entire body and significantly changes not only the physiological functions such as breathing, heartbeat, pulse, and EEG, but tosses the whole body back and forth, causes cramps in individual limbs, and so forth.

It is likewise significant that in the various prior lives certain specific characteristics manifest themselves that frequently have little resemblance to the character and behavior pattern of the subject. In many instances, even the voice changes so markedly that it does not bear the slightest resemblance to the "normal voice" of the subject. I have played tape recordings for various people in which an almost sixty-year-old woman relives her childhood and upon asking these people to judge the age of the owner of the voice, they all judged her to be a girl fifteen to twenty years of age. On one occasion, the tender voice of a young female patient turned to a coarse, male voice during the session.

The following case was particularly interesting. A patient relived his last previous life in which, as a German soldier during World War I, he was stabbed in the left hip by a soldier while storming a French stronghold and died as a result of this wound. During the next consultation, this patient told me that since birth he had had a mark on his left hip that at first glance appeared to be a healed scar, but that must have been caused by a change in pigmentation of his skin. Only at home, when he mentioned this to his wife, did both realize that this was the location of that wound for which no basis was found in this life. Such an isolated incident might not be considered as proof by many and, as is frequently the case, might be dismissed as "coincidence." But as much as a decade ago, the American reincarnation researcher, Professor Ian Stevenson, published results of numerous cases in which he showed that scars had apparently been caused during a previous life.

There are more phenomena that, in my opinion, cannot be readily explained by the above-mentioned hypotheses. It is possible to have a subject write during a session. In such instances, we have seen not only changes in handwriting, but depending on the period in question, complete changes in the styles of script in which the subjects wrote fluently during the session, even though their eyes were closed.

Samples written by a twenty-year-old secretary reliving her life in ancient Egypt, in the twentieth year of the Pharaoh, were particularly impressive. The next question that arises might be whether the subject can also speak the ancient language— and he can! Of course, the entire interview is carried on in German in order to assure continual contact. The asking of questions by me and the answering in the same language is laid down by me at the beginning of the experiment through the power of suggestion so that the rapport between the subject and me is not lost when the communication ends. During the session, however, I can command the subject to give certain answers in the "original" language. This command is usually obeyed, although at first the foreign language is not spoken fluently or with ease. During subsequent sessions, however, improvement can be obtained.

Thus far, unfortunately, I have not had the time during a series of interviews to develop an ancient language to such an extent that the subject can speak it as a regular foreign language during his waking state. Such experiments are, however, planned for the near future, not only with regard to languages, but also with reference to other talents, such as playing the piano.

One session with the above-mentioned subject, who believed she had been a dancer in the temple of the goddess Isis in ancient Egypt, was very impressive. I had her rise in her hypnotic state and perform her temple dance with her eyes closed. While I cannot of my own knowledge judge whether the dance she danced was identical to the temple dance as performed in ancient Egypt, it was fascinating to watch her sultry movements and the exact play of the hands and fingers that are typical of Eastern cultures. This dance, artistically perfect in every movement, and performed effortlessly in deep hypnotic sleep, is an accomplishment that can hardly be dismissed as an incidental, currently injected talent.

Let us summarize. New, self-contained characteristics and personality traits appear; sociocultural connections with long-forgotten ages are presented in detail, far beyond the scope of general education (as in weights, measures, and monetary values); there are changes in voice, changes in handwriting, former wounds that are still visible in the skin, knowledge of ancient languages and writing, spontaneous appearance of abilities that were not learned in this life. How are all these phenomena explained? Are they fantasy or a conglomeration of what has been read or learned? Perhaps some variation of extrasensory perception or an ESP phenomenon?

If it were a matter of a few instances in which these phenomena occurred, they could be explained away easily with any old parapsychological hypotheses. But I have been able to carry out these experiments with almost anyone, whether he believes in them or considers them nonsense from the start—always with the same results. In this way, I fulfill one of the necessary requirements of our science, which demands that the experiment be reproducible at any time. The experiment is repeated daily— it does not depend on external circumstances. I need nothing more than a couch and a subject who is willing to have the experiment performed on him and sufficient time to slowly train the subject in the technique of regression. The experiment cannot always be carried out in one or two hours, but this should not incur serious criticism because other types of experiments also require time.

What is important for our argument is that the experiment can be repeated and reproduced at any time desired and that the same basic phenomenon appears every time: A person experiences something that he describes as his life, even though it may be far back in time. A living individual describes his death, his existence after death; tells of his new connection with a body, describes his impressions as an embryo, and relives the pains of his birth.

After the session, when the individual is fully awake, something happens that is even more surprising than the session itself: the subject continues to recall his former life and speaks of these recollections in the same matter-of-fact manner with which another person talks of yesterday's events. The recollections brought forth during the session are relived in a waking condition with the same feeling of personal identity as recollections pertaining to one's current life.

This is an important point because a person can easily distinguish between a dream and reality. Even though a dream, while one is dreaming, can appear to be as real as life, the moment the dreamer awakens and realizes that he is awake, he knows that what he "experienced" was only a dream and he can generally distinguish with certainty between this and his recollections of what he has actually experienced in real life. Every normal person knows for sure whether he ever fell into the water as a child or whether he only dreamed that he fell in.

This ability to distinguish ought also to be conceded a hypnotized individual. It is particularly noticeable in this respect that my subjects combine the contents of their sessions with what they have actually experienced. In addition, the subjects, while awake, begin to describe further details of their "former" lives, details that were not even discussed during the session. Thus a hypnosis session is frequently followed by a conversational session in a waking state during which we obtain further information about an earlier life. These sessions are sometimes extremely productive, since the activity and pace of speaking are much greater than during hypnosis and its attendant passiveness.

The hypnotic session somewhat resembles the opening of a door that leads to remembrance. Once it is open and if it is not closed again during hypnosis, it will remain open for all time, and the rooms of remembrance beyond it can be entered at any time, even in a waking state. We know this from our own daily lives. We forget a certain incident—we try to remember it—we can't remember it—there is no entrance. If someone comes along to give us direction ("Wasn't that the day we were celebrating Uncle Otto's fiftieth birthday?"), a door to our recollection is suddenly opened, and soon we recall the entire story that we had forgotten. We observe a very similar mechanism in our regression experiments. We need only open up an access route in order to be able to explore further at will. This access route is created by our experiment, but the phenomena themselves are not bound by the experimental situations.

THE REINCARNATION HYPOTHESIS

Having attempted to describe the weakness of previous hypotheses, I should like to be permitted to explain what I consider to be the best and most obvious explanation of our phenomenon. I shall start with what this experiment actually has to offer, without forcefully adding or subtracting anything, without giving it meaning or interpretation.

Why should it not be what all hypnosis subjects say and feel it is: a chain of former lives that have been forgotten and are now being remembered? Why do we struggle with such vehemence against this simple train of thought that under the name of "reincarnation" (Greek = reembodiment) has for ages been accepted as a matter of course by the majority of human beings? All major religions and the majority of all philosophers teach reembodiment. (In Christianity, reincarnation was not abolished until the Council of Constantinople in the year 553!)

From the point of view of physical science, the teaching of reincarnation appears devious and unfamiliar to wide circles of the Western world. This is understandable, because if one begins by saying axiomatically that consciousness exists only in conjunction with matter and that, in fact, the consciousness process is only a product of some procedure of metabolism, the theory of reembodiment must appear absurd. What can be reembodied, when there exists nothing but bodies?

Whether the scientific axiom that consciousness processes are dependent on matter be correct or erroneous, it would appear useful to set aside this axiom temporarily in order to be able to understand the concept of reincarnation without prejudice. The basis for this is the classic three-part division of body, soul, and spirit. These three members are clearly distinguishable qualitatively, but are interchangeable with one another. According to this view, the body is nothing but matter, which is the only remaining part of a person after he dies. The spirit corresponds to the life principle, or simply "life," without individual or personal character and is universal and indestructible. In the soul, we find that part of the human being that we call "self-assurance," the agent that stamps individuality.

When these three factors are combined into one entity, we have a human being. (Here we shall temporarily disregard the fact that this conformity may also be valid outside of human beings in other kingdoms of nature.) Life combines with an "individual" soul, and both form a material body according to their plan. The living soul in this case would be the information carrier whose objectives take shape within the body and become formally visible. In this manner, body functions would be the expression of consciousness.

Science, however, considers consciousness an expression of body functions. Here we have two contrary interpretations, and there may be good arguments for both. In my opinion, the first is more likely because our experience with matter indicates that simple matter never produces consciousness processes. Why should "human matter" be an exception? Even if we accept this exception, the act of dying is quite remarkable. Why should a body produce sixty years of consciousness only to discontinue it suddenly?

As opposed to this, death is much more explainable with our hypothesis. If the soul were to form the body, the concept that we are accustomed to designating as death would appear upon the occasion of the separation of soul and body. Surmising this procedure, people have always spoken of it in the vernacular as "he is departed from us," "he has given up the ghost," and so on. All these expressions stem from the fact that "something" has left the body of the living being and has left only the corpse behind.

This lifeless body can hardly have been the producer of what we call life, consciousness, personality, and individuality. This body was the shell, the executive organ. A television set requires a program in order to present an opera, but it cannot produce the opera itself. If we remove the program, a dead, silent box remains. It is eminently important that we free ourselves of the need to identify the individuality of a human being with his body. He who is willing to at least try this step toward changing his thinking will have no difficulty in following our reincarnation hypothesis.

If we believe it to be possible for the soul to exist alone without basic matter, at least our experiments showed the various consecutive connections of a particular soul (individuality) with bodies. Or, expressed in another way, an individual "ego" rhythmically runs through a phase of a corporal existence, frees itself from this shell, only to enter into a new connection with matter after a period of noncorporal existence. Here the "ego" constantly remains the same, while the bodies vary from life to life.

If this theory appears somewhat far-fetched to those with different patterns of thought, it nevertheless confirms exactly what everyone reports about himself when through the technique of hypnosis we release the "memory barriers." Is it so much easier to believe that all these people feed us the same lies or that they all have the same foolish dreams, or might it not simply be possible that the facts are as reported by them in response to questioning? If we knew nothing about our former incarnations previously, it is only because no one ever asked about them. No other hypothesis appears so simple and obvious to me as that of reincarnation. If once more we check against this pattern phenomena that might crop up, we shall see that no contradictions will appear.

Thus far, I have scarcely mentioned the one phenomenon that in the meantime has become the focal point of my work: the connection between psychic symptoms in the current life and traumatic experiences in earlier incarnations. Once I recognized this connection, it was only a small step to develop from these fascinating experiments a new therapeutic method, the results of which caused me to formulate the concept of reincarnation therapy.

−47

Reincarnation
Therapy

Explore the stream of your soul;
whence and how you arrived.
ZOROASTER

Record of a Therapy Session, April 1975 *

S: I am so hungry and thirsty [*moans*], I don't know, I think
they are going to execute me.

H: First tell me what you did. Tell me everything very
slowly.

S: What I did? Well, I don't know. I did something to Afrah,
I don't know, Afrah-Afrah, Afrahmus.

H: What did you do?

S: Afrah, Afrah, I don't know, Afrahmus.

---

* The record of this session begins somewhat abruptly because I only
turned on the tape recorder when I noticed a sudden regression into a
previous life. I had simply requested my hypnotized patient to go back to
the cause of her fear. The reliving of the incarnation in this case was not
the result of suggestion and was neither expected nor intended.

H: What did you do?

S: Afrahmus, I slandered him, accused him, no, they claim I accused him because—I wanted to poison him—there were two or three men, they have a sort of red robe, and they have golden stripes, as if they were painted—the golden stripes are on the robes—and they are wearing peculiar hats—strange, they look like helmets—like helmets on suits of armor—the color looks like—like tin.

H: What is the color?

S: Tin, tin or pewter, pewter vessels, pewter vessels, copper—pewter vessels, it is so, it is so wide, and then the rays bounce off this helmet, it looks almost like a crown, but it isn't—every one of these men is wearing this crown.

H: Who are these men?

S: There are three.

H: Which three?

S: They are bodyguards.

H: Whose?

S: Well, they—I don't know—he is wearing a white robe, very long, sometimes he wears it short—he—

H: Who is he?

S: He is so tall, what is his name? He is slender—what is his name? Rrrr, with an R, no—that is the Imperator—he is an Imperator—he is [*moans*].

H: What is the matter?

S: I have trouble getting air.

H: Why?

S: I don't know, he is the one! He sent my husband, he sent my husband into the arena, he sent him into the arena, that I know.

H: What did he do?

S: Yes, he sent him into the arena.

H: Why?

S: Well, that is, because he was a Christian [*moans*]. I don't know his name—Augustinus—maybe—there are so many—I am afraid.

H: Of whom?

S: I am afraid, I don't know.

H: Of that man?

S: No, I, I—they will take me—they will take me away, too—I am so afraid, I am terribly afraid—everything is so dark and smells musty [*moans*]—there is nothing on the floors, not even straw, and they are throwing me in there—

H: What is your name?

S: [*Cries*] I don't know my name. I don't know, I don't, oh, I don't know.

H: Very well, what happens next? Who brought you here?

S: A, Afrahmus, Afrahmus.

H: Who is he?

S: A Latin, I don't know why, no—that is from someone, I don't know where he is from—I don't know.

H: Is that a name? Afrahmus?

S: I, I am, I know, I am so afraid, because he has this face; it looks terrible, the hair, it is a manly face, the hair seems to stand on end—and the way he laughs—and his teeth—he looks horrible—I am afraid of him—I am afraid of him—he is the one who is to execute me!

H: What did you do?

S: With the wood, the wooden door, with the wood—I want to get something for someone—poison—because I have to go through the door—through the big, wooden door, I must get through this door, I must get through, I must get through the door.

H: Why must you get through the door?

S: It is very important—

H: What are you planning to do?

S: I want to deliver something. I want to deliver something!

H: What do you want to deliver?

S: Hm, that is an examiner, I can't tell you that, that's the way it is.

H: A poison?

S: Yes, that is something, that will do him in!

H: Whom?

S: I don't know, it is supposed to be—no, that is from Afrahmus, his brother, the brother murderer—

H: Tell me, keep talking, speak, keep talking!

S: Oh, yes, I am so afraid [*very frightened, faltering and crying*] I am so afraid, they will do away with me.

H: Who wants to do away with you?

S: I must do something, I must do something—

H: Tell me your plans very slowly—what do you want to do? What must you do?

S: I must—that is the Imperator!

H: Who is the Imperator?

S: I don't know—I know I see him, but those are the letters MVN.

H: Once more, louder!

S: VMN, MVNI, I don't know what that is.

H: Read it to me again, just as you said it now. Once more, loud, how does it start?

S: XMVNI, III, I—but there is something else—they will crucify me—

H: Why will they do that?

S: Because they are persecuting Christians.

H: Are you a Christian?

S: Yes, my husband was one and so am I.

H: What happened to your husband? Tell me!

S: They left him with the wild animal—Afrahmus.

H: Who is Afrahmus?

S: I don't know.

H: Do you like him or not?

S: Yes, I like him.

H: Afrahmus, is that your husband?

S: He's handsome, beautiful curly hair, brown locks, and a very short robe—the one, the men, the three men, they have one that is longer, it reaches almost to the knees, and his covers the ankle, and the Imperator's—his is floor-length and white with gold, and he plays the harp, no, it's not really a harp, it's called something else.

H: What is it called?

S: I don't know, I can't think of it now.

H: I shall count to three, then you will remember it. One, two, three.

S: Fet, no not Feder, Feder isn't right, either. Feder, Feder, that is my name—Feder, Feder, Feder—I don't know, that's Cyrillic, no, what am I saying—I don't know why—Cyrillic is Feder—Feder is Cyrillic—I don't know—that's just part of it.

H: Where do you live? In what city, in what country?

S: I don't know the name, I know it's called—the houses—there are the big houses with the MVN—I don't know—Po—no, that's not the Po—po—vonde—no, that's really not a city, that's not a city, this square. That is the square, that is a square and many little squares—that is not a city.

H: What is this square called?

S: I don't know, I don't know. It's beautiful!

H: You just mentioned a name, or the beginning of a name!

S: Yes, no, that's not it—Potenas, Potenas—no, that's not it.

H: What was the name you just mentioned?

S: Pontenas.

H: Is that the name of a town?

S: No, that is a square, that is a square, it is a growing—it is very pretty, the scenery—it is lovely and green and it's beautiful there—and they have—we live there with an old man—we have lived there a long time—yes—

H: Who, you and your husband?

S: Yes, the family, the whole family.

H: About how old are you?

S: I know—seventeen—possibly seventeen years old.

H: You are married?

S: Yes, he is my husband.

H: And you are Christians?

S: Yes, we are Christians [*sobs*].

H: Is it dangerous to be a Christian?

S: Yes.

H: Why?

S: They are killed.

H: The Christians?

S: Yes.

H: By whom?

S: Hm—they are legionnaires.

H: I beg your pardon?

S: Legionnaires—they persecute us.

H: Who is persecuting you?

S: The legionnaires—yes, they followed us to this house, and we like them—this is a friend of my father's; my father is dead—they carried my mother away—Afrahmus.

H: Who is that?

S: He is a young warrior.

H: From where do you know him?

S: I met him—at my uncle's house.

H: But this is not your husband?

S: I don't know, he is not, no, he is not yet my husband.

H: Do you love each other?

S: Yes, very much—and he wants—he wants to be baptized. They always baptize there.

H: Where?

S: They baptize every evening.

H: Where?

S: They baptize in my uncle's house, that is the secret, it's called—it is a villa—and everything is green, all around, and we meet under the pretext of having a banquet, but we celebrate the Holy Mass, no, a sacrifice—a sacrificial worship—not a mass.

H: What do you sacrifice?

S: Sirenus, Sirenus, Sirenus, I think it is Sirenus—those are sacrificial offerings—and Sirenus sees to it that no one disturbs us—the old man is there, too, and there are young girls, virgins—and they are all waiting for news—because there will be war, yes, there will be war, there will be war.

H: Against whom?

S: Because there will be war—against there—oh, I am afraid.

H: What are you afraid of?

S: There are so many faces—and they brought a writing—but it is a foreign writing—from a foreign country—far away—and no one can read this writing—and now they will—Sirenus will be [*cries*] yes, because—someone is coming—I can't—I have to be quiet [*moans and cries*]—soldiers are coming—and they are looking for us—da—daa—daarints—darrint—darinnts—

H: What word is that?

S: Oh, it is between two hills, Darinnt—Darinnts.

H: Where is that?

S: [*cries*] That is where everyone is crucified.

H: How do you know that?

S: Because I see it, I see it [*cries*].

H: You need have no fear! Tell me what happens next.

S: I see so many letters—but I can't pronounce them—they are so strange—we have to solve a problem—and if we do not solve it, we are crucified. But it is impossible to solve this problem.

H: What sort of problem is it?

S: Oh—wood from which blood flows, that is the wood from which blood flows.

H: Can you explain that better? What is the nature of the problem?

S: Break the wood from which blood flows, bring it before my eyes, bring me the wood from which blood flows.

H: What sort of wood is that, from which blood flows?

S: It is dark wood; I don't know what it is called, it is dark wood.

H: Do you know it?

S: It is possible, it is possible.

H: Tell me the problem once more. What is it you must do?

S: Break the wood that bleeds, and bring it before my eyes so that I can see, so I can see, and the light, so that—I can see and the light will turn red and the sky will turn red. I know—

the wood comes from between the two hills in Darinnts, the wood is found between the two hills.

H: How do you know that?

S: It is the wood from which stakes and crosses are made—that they tie us to. The wood with which they impale us, so that the blood flows.

H: And you cannot solve the problem?

S: We would like to and are close to it, but they are getting ahead of us, they are getting ahead of us, no, we could solve the problem, but we are at war, yes, and there is the sky, it is so blood—red, that is that—we are supposed to ask, where is the wood from which blood flows when it is broken. Bring it before my eyes, so I can see the sky red. I am afraid—and I know that if I go on—they will catch me.

H: Why are you alone? Where are the others?

S: Where? In the mountains, is the mountains perhaps, I don't know, perhaps in the mountains, in the mountains behind the hills, yes, it is before the gates.

H: Whose gates?

S: Of our Romanum.

H: Whose gates?

S: That is a Romanum.

H: What is a Romanum?

S: Where we all live.

H: That is called Romanum?

S: Yes, that is a Romanum, because they called it that, Romanum, but another name, another name—I am always afraid—if only it were over—and Afrahmus—I have something, with which I can do someone a favor. I will bring him, I will bring him something that looks like—yes—like manna, but it is not, it only looks like it—and he will be dead after he eats it—and he will be dead, but it will probably end before that.

H: Who will be dead after he has eaten it?

S: He is a friend, a friend of—I don't know—I can't remember the name—I know how he looks, but I don't know his name.

-55

H: What is his function, what does he do?

S: He oppresses everyone, every human being, he makes them slaves, and he rules a large empire, a large empire, he is very powerful, very powerful, but he hates all Christians, he hates all Christians!

H: He is very powerful—is he a king, an emperor?

S: No, no, he is the Imperator, he is an Imperator, he is the— no, emperor—he has many titles, he has many titles—Augustus, Augustinus, Augustus, no, Augustinus, yes, Augustinus. He hates all Christians, he hates all Christians from Romanus, it is to be cleansed, Romanus, and a noble race is to take over—and no dogs like these Christians—car—carn—will be sacrificed—carne.

H: What will be sacrificed?

S: I don't know—carn—carne—carne—yes, many are bringing animals, sheep.

H: What are you doing now? You are going to poison someone?

S: Yes, I, that is—I am baking it inside a bread.

H: What sort of poison is it? Where did you get it?

S: There is a chamber, from a heal—no—a, with a—there is a—with flowers and plants.

H: That is where you got the poison?

S: No, I am going to get it, I will steal it.

H: You know it is poison?

S: I swear it.

H: What do you swear?

S: I swear it is poison, I have killed him!

H: Whom?

S: Sssirenus, Sirenus.

H: Did he eat the bread?

S: Yes.

H: Was he supposed to eat it?

S: Yes, he was supposed to eat it.

H: Why?

S: So he would not betray us, but he didn't do it.

H: What didn't he do?

S: He did not betray us, but I thought he had betrayed us.

H: Who is Sirenus?

S: [*cries*] He is—I think—he is a brother—my brother—I swear it—

H: What do you swear?

S: I want to do penance—I don't know—I must do it.

H: What must you do?

S: Raise three fingers! I must swear before many people, and they will crucify me.

H: Why will they crucify you?

S: Not because I am a Christian.

H: But?

S: Because I committed murder, an assassination with poison. He was going to betray us, and Taurus said—Taurus is the man who ordered me to bake the poison. I will give him manna. I bake it and it is dark and long and shiny; it is like a fruit. The poison comes from a fruit, from a fruit that—I don't know what it's called. It comes from, no—yes, it does, from a foreign country far away and is dark brown, almost as dark as ebony— almost black and it is long, very long and thin, and when you taste it, it tastes like something that looks just like that. That is why it is not noticed when I bake it into the bread—it is a custom with us. At this time, we always bake something into the bread.

H: What time is this?

S: We bake it into the bread!

H: At what time? What do you call this time?

S: An inverted T—I don't know.

H: What is the significance of this time? Is it a festival?

S: Yes it is a festival, a festival of resurrection, and that is when we bake that way. But the fruit is not the real thing, it is poison.

H: And you are baking this poisonous fruit into the bread?

S: Yes, because Taurus ordered me to.

H: You would not have done it otherwise?

S: No, I don't think so.

H: Who is Taurus?

S: Taurus is a soldier, no, he is a scribe, a scribe for a master, in a house.

H: Is he a Christian?

S: He says he is a Christian. Yes, he is a Christian.

H: And for whom is this bread intended?

S: For Sirenus.

H: Is Sirenus a Christian?

S: He is a Christian, but he is a traitor, he is a traitor.

H: And he is eating this bread?

S: Yes. I bring him the basket, a wicker basket. The basket is very small, but it has a long handle, a handle to carry it, and I stand before him and next to me are two little children. I give him the bread. He is standing in front of a big building—it is a —a—it is a—I don't know—I am standing before a huge vault— yes, now he eats the bread, he eats the bread and he is going to die—and he looks at me questioningly—very questioningly and says nothing—he only looks questioningly and with big eyes—I don't know—what shall I do? What shall I do? [*cries*] Brother— I am . . .

H: Tell me everything you are thinking!

S: I am upset, I can't get air, and I can't breathe.

H: Why? Just keep talking.

S: I did not want to do it, he was not the one, he was not the one.

H: How do you know that now?

S: Because of the way he looked at me—so surprised and so questioningly, he couldn't have done it, he didn't do it, he was not the one—I know he didn't do it—I am going home and try —but the guards are coming after me, the guards are after me. Yes, and I see my uncle's house; he is standing there and looking very sad, he is wearing a long, long robe, a long dress, and he is standing there looking at me; he looks at me and says nothing, and I can see it in his eyes, he is very sad at what I have done— because I trusted Taurus—and he turns and walks away. I am going before a tribunal.

H: Where are you going?

S: I am going before a tribunal and will be . . . I am standing in a large hall, it is like a church, I am standing here and there are many men, they will pronounce the judgment—I know some of them—former friends of my father's—yes, I know some of them—I confess, I confess, I swear I am a murderess—I am a murderess, yes, Taurus, Taurus, where will you go now, he will go where the sun is blood red, and I shall go into the valley . . .

H: Just keep talking quietly!

S: I am afraid, but not for myself; what will happen to the others now—what will happen to them? And then Afrahmus, he despises me—he never wants to see me again—never again. The men are all so loud, asking me questions.

H: What are they asking?

S: They want me to tell them where the Christians celebrate their secret masses—where they worship—they want me to talk about what Christians do and why they do it—they are laughing and ridiculing me—saying I am not a Christian—because I am a murderess—a brother murderess—and that is why they will crucify me, not because I am a Christian. There are so many who say they love God, but they don't love Him, they are not permitted to love anyone other than the emperor—he has been doing that a long time, an XV—he has been doing that for eighteen months, or is it days—no, he persecutes Christians and night and day he sends soldiers into their houses to find their hiding places and then has them murdered. It is terrible, they want me to deny my God—they want me to swear—to renounce my faith —I won't do it—they want me to renounce God, Christ, I am going to lose my life, so be it, it doesn't matter for what reason, I know I must die, and I want to, because I regret—[*cries*]. Taurus is going where the days are three-quarters filled, three-quarters filled—more than half—he is going to a land where the days are white for one quarter of the circle and the other part is in the dark—night—yes? I see the lines and the circles, so many lines and circles, but I can't read, that is why I don't understand —I cannot read—I don't enjoy that privilege—men—all of high

−*59*

rank—they can read and some of them are scribes, just like Taurus. But I cannot read and I cannot write, but I know about plants—that will be my downfall—Taurus contrived that, very cleverly—yes, he came into our house and said he was a Christian. Under this pretext he gained our confidence—and I believed him because I was blind, and killed my brother. He said nothing, but asked in such a manner, and raised his eyes—I am being put into a dungeon, I am being led there, it is so twisted, I have to go far down, and there I am chained so that I can no longer swear and no longer regret—hm—they are putting something on my hands and on my ankles—I don't know what they call it—the blacksmith does it—I am put in irons—and I have to wait—then we are led away—I don't know what will happen now, I am afraid, I am terribly afraid of what will happen. There are so many women, and they all have long hair, and now their hair is being burned off, yes, burned off, yes, they are tying us to the cross with ropes and starting a fire, I am afraid, I am afraid . . .

H: You will be very calm and tell us what else is happening.

S: I am afraid.

H: You will feel nothing. You will only see it. You will breathe calmly and evenly and tell me what else is happening—tell me!

S: They are gathering wood and putting it down, but they are not lighting it yet, because we have to stay there until the sky is colored red—but I don't care anymore, because . . .

H: Tell me more.

S: I am coming, I am going away, I am going away from myself, I am going further and further away . . .

H: You are going away from yourself?

S: Yes, I am going away from myself, hm.

H: Can you still see anything?

S: I don't know—no—it is beautiful, yes, I see our bodies—all of them—and nothing hurts anymore—it is beautiful!

H: What do you feel now?

S: It's just like gliding—always further away—the voice—is

—world-encompassing—it is freedom—I notice—I am everything and nothing—I am here.

H: What are you saying?

S: I am here and I am there, but I am there—that is, I am something that escaped out of myself. Now I am pure and clean, now I am—it is a powerful feeling—I am, hm—but I feel nothing, see nothing, hear nothing, only it is I, alone—it is nothing—I shall withdraw.

H: Where to?

S: I don't know, everything is music there, yes, in the sphere, I don't know—there is no name for it, but it is beautiful! I am waiting for something, I am waiting for something—because I feel it is becoming tighter—like a spiral.

H: Good, but before you examine these things more closely, let us go forward in time, constantly forward, without looking at the details. One century after another is floating by, until we reach the year 1900.

S: Yes, I am entering a body, my ego is going into a body, into a body, yes, it has so many twists and turns until it gets inside, I am wondering whether life is fleeing, whether life is leaving, I don't know. The air . . .

H: No, the air cannot leave. You are being born!

S: Yes, it is pleasant! Now I know, now I know!

H: What do you know?

S: That I am becoming a human, I know, I know, I am about to become a being, I know it.

H: You will experience a deep calm from now on. There are no more fears.

S: That is true, I know.

H: What do you feel?

S: Yes, peace, peace and happiness because of the peace—and oceanic, world-encompassing, no, encompassing worlds; it is a sensation so wide and so large and so broad, it is not a feeling of space, it is difficult to describe—truly wonderful [*laughs*].

She lies there and beams. Mrs Inge S. from Nuremberg,

twenty-eight years old, married, housewife, has just completed her thirteenth session. She is my patient. She did not want to know about her prior lives, but wanted to be freed of a large number of symptoms that had been severely troubling her for several years. When she came to me, she had discontinued a one-and-a-half-year psychotherapy treatment because of some objections. Her symptoms were far-reaching and to some extent very unusual. She had depressions and on occasion suffered attacks of terrible fear. She was unable to leave the house alone and was afraid of people. She particularly hated all women and had the feeling that she had to beat pregnant women because "every pregnant woman is a murderess." She could not look into a mirror, and for that reason had not been to a beauty parlor for years. Combing her hair caused her great difficulty because she could not find the part, "the middle of life." When she passed people whom she did not like, she held her breath so that she did not need to share the air with them. When she succeeded in leaving her house, it was not possible for her to return home. All symptoms were mixed with religious ideas; she spoke of the original sin, of the fear of being discovered, and suggested that "there was something that had to be said."

I began the therapy by selecting individual symptoms during the hypnotic state and allowing their emotional content to be experienced. This emotion serves as a sort of guideline, like a red thread, in that I ask the patient to go back in time with this emotion until he finds an incident or experience in which this feeling was present. This technique of going back along the path of an emotion is quite time-saving and productive. The patient himself comes upon events, all of which are similar because they have a central emotional theme. He who has never experienced this type of regression will probably have difficulty imagining it.

In a normal case, with a patient who requires hypnosis or daydream technique, this regression usually takes place in an optical manner. The patient lies down with his eyes closed, experiences a pleasant relaxation, and sees experiences transpire before his eyes like a film. He watches these pictures and at the same time reports on what he is seeing. The inner relation to the happening depends on the depth of the hypnosis and the personality of the patient.

In deep hypnosis, what the patient sees becomes an experience at the same time; the patient experiences the situation he happens to see with all his emotions, without realizing that he is lying on a couch in a therapy session. If the hypnosis is not deep, the individual knows exactly where he is, but nevertheless sees his earlier experiences like a film. What is crucial to this technique is the fact that the patient is not looking for recollections and is not actively rummaging through his memory so that he will find only what is more or less known to him anyhow, but rather that in a completely passive manner he submits himself to whatever may arise. Pictures, therefore, are not produced, they simply appear. In this way, this method also offers direct access to the suppressed, unconscious experiences.

By this method, we can quickly look for important traumata in the very early childhood years. This search for a trauma or several traumata is the basic ingredient of my procedure; it is not new and is the basis for almost all deep psychological therapy. This stems from the fact that an unhappy experience in the past may be the cause of a symptom that because of its unpleasant nature is expelled from one's consciousness.

Now it may be possible to expel the recollection of an experience, but not its emotional portion. This emotional part of the experience remains in a freely fluctuating state after the expulsion and on a later occasion, which through some similarity may recall the expelled experience, will be projected into the new situation. Thus a symptom is born.

Therapy must reverse this process. The goal of therapy is therefore to bring back to conscious knowledge the experience that has been expelled and forgotten. If this procedure is successful, the symptom disappears because the patient can dissolve the symptomatic projection by recognizing that this feeling belongs to an event far in the past. He learns to put his emotions, which were momentarily stimulated, back into their proper time sequence.

We see here the enormous importance of time. In the final analysis, a neurosis is created when a person is unable to place his emotions into a proper time sequence.

Let us assume that a young woman is afraid of all men. She herself does not know why, and recognizes this fear as foolish, but experiences the fear, nevertheless. The reason for this could be, for example, that when she was five years old, some strange man accosted her on a path in the woods, undressed her, and touched her genitals. (Such an incident is called a trauma; Greek= wound.) This incident at that time aroused great fear, and because of fear and shame, she never told anyone about it. In time, she forgot this experience. However, forgetting is only an apparent solution, because forgetting eliminates nothing, but simply prevents something from being seen. The fear that she connected with the man at that time remains.

In our example, the young woman experiences fear every time she comes in contact with men. We speak here of restimulation. This means that by means of an external stimulus, the feeling connected with an earlier experience, which somewhat resembles the current stimulus, is newly released. The woman in our example, even with the best of intentions, will not lose her fear of men until she recognizes the real cause. However, should it be possible for her to consciously recognize the fact that her current fear is actually the fear she experienced as a five-year-old, her projection will disappear. She can now place her fear in the proper time sequence. Her problem therefore was time confusion.

At the start, I know only a patient's symptom. I suspect that some unfortunate experience (trauma) some time in the past is the cause—but neither of us, neither the patient nor I, knows the trauma. What is certain is that everything the patient can tell me (frequently a great deal) has nothing to do with the symptom—because this is known material—otherwise he could not tell me about it. Unfortunately, what is known does not lead us to the symptom. The problem is to develop a technique that will help us find the unknown. Any technique that helps us find what we are looking for is a good technique.

In psychoanalysis, one uses free association, interpretation of dreams, and other similar methods. The remedy I use is hypnosis in order to open the door to the unknown and then follow the red thread until this thread leads me to the experience we are seeking. This red thread is emotion or feeling. It is recognized by means of the symptom and must have been present during this event.

Thus outlined, this method works very well, but in reality things do not always go as smoothly. This repressed material resists being lifted into the consciousness and it is the struggle against this resistance that takes the greatest amount of time in psychotherapeutic treatment.

Here we obviously ran up against an energic problem. C. G. Jung in his early psychiatric studies developed a complex model that I believe appropriately explains the energic happening. In his treatise *The Emotion Emphasis Complex*, Jung describes how other complexes are built molecularly alongside the ego complex, and how each attempts to grow in intensity: "All psychic energy turns toward the complex at the expense of the remaining psychic materials." ("Complex" here means a higher union of various mental images held together by one emotional state.) We can picture such a complex as somewhat like a constantly growing crystal. A random emotional experience, as time goes on, surrounds itself with emotionally similar incidents and so becomes more and more laden with energy. This growth in energy can go so far that it approaches in intensity the normally higher-ranked ego complex or perhaps even threatens to surpass it.

Repressed and forgotten incidents each form complexes distinguished from one another by their energic strength. For this energy load, we use the concept of a "charge." We speak of a "high charge" when a complex or group of experiences has grown very large and so contains a highly emotional state.

C. G. Jung in his early years had already examined and described the theoretical principles of the emotion emphasis complex and its disturbing influence on the thinking and behavior of the experimental human in his association experiments. The procedure in this experiment is simple: the subject is given a so-called stimulus word that he is to answer with the first word that comes to mind (association), for example, tree-root or kiss —love. From the nature of the reaction word and the reaction time between stimulus word and answer, one may determine whether or not the stimulus word touched a complex.

Jung later enlarged on these experiments by simultaneously measuring the galvanic skin response of the subject. This procedure, which through modern electronics has become considerably simpler than in Jung's time, measures with relative numerical accuracy what we have called the "charge." The following principle has evolved: the greater the "charge" in a complex, the less likely the possibility that it can become conscious knowledge. This relationship is known to everyone by the familiar example of various animal phobia. The greater the fear of a particular animal, the less one wants to see it. But even the process of becoming conscious is really nothing more than a "viewing." An experience that in the past was so unpleasant or emotionally disturbing that it was repressed has to be viewed again in order to bring it back into consciousness. The viewing, however, brings back with it the entire emotional impression, and this is exactly what the consciousness fears, especially if the emotional experience was highly charged.

Here we have the reason why the finding of the trauma we seek is usually not so simple. Consciousness defends itself, and this resistance is a defense mechanism that protects the ego from an emotional overflow so that a too powerful complex with all its energy does not suddenly explode like a bomb. For if the charge was great at the time of repression, it has meanwhile been enlarged many times over in that the complex has attached similar experiences to itself. What can, therefore, be done in order on the one hand to make the traumatic complex known and on the other hand to not exclude the valuable safety mechanism of defense?

Let us return once more to the example of the animal phobia. We shall imagine someone who is terribly afraid of snakes. As soon as he hears the word "snake," he feels ill. Pictures of snakes are revolting to him. Were you to come up from behind and hang a huge, living snake around his neck, you could certainly release a tremendous shock that would more likely increase his fear than free him from it. If the latter is your goal, you will probably proceed more slowly and carefully. Perhaps you will at first tell him something about the positive side of snakes, then show him a few pictures, and in this manner try to reconcile him step by step with the object of his fear. When you finally show him a real snake from a distance, he will probably turn away at first, then look at it a bit longer until slowly and gradually he becomes used to it.

This procedure, which is probably clear to everyone, is today applied frequently in behavior therapy under the designation of "systematic desensitizing," especially with phobia. In this connection, however, we must make something else clear because our problem is not animal phobia, but a "complex phobia." For this reason, our procedure in the trauma search had best be oriented toward similar points of view.

If we picture our complex as a large molecule, the trauma we seek is located in its center as the nucleus, the original experience, around which are grouped, like individual atoms, all the similar experiences that have occurred in the meantime. This complex is easy to find because the symptom is its expression. In accordance with the above-described procedure, we will not try to immediately crack the nut forcefully, but will start with the outer shell. In practice, this means, for example, that the patient for the first time reports an incident that occurred during the past week and that thematically or emotionally pertains to the complex.

When I speak of reporting, this is not exactly what I mean. In our case, we try to have the patient relive the experience rather than deliver an intellectual report as a pure feat of memory. There is a tremendous difference between my saying, "Last month, my mother-in-law visited me and we had an argument about the children," and placing myself back in time and experiencing it: "My mother-in-law is entering the house; she is wearing a green dress. I see her entering the room and hear her say to . . ."

Through the technique of hypnosis and thinking in terms of filmstrips, it is rather easy to relive a situation even when it goes far back in time. If every experience is an atom in our complex molecule, the pertinent atom, when an incident is relived, is unloaded and loses its charge. Thus, by going back along the time axis, reliving all situations and seeing once again the component parts of the complex, the large molecule can be made to slowly decrease in size. The further one goes back, the more incidents appear that the patient could not have "normally" recalled. Here the patient learns, much to his surprise, that "not being able to remember" in actuality is "not wanting to remember" and that there is no forgetting.

If this procedure of making known continues, sooner or later one must come upon the nucleus and reach the actual trauma. This incident can now also be made known because its "charge" has in the meantime shrunk to a bearable size, and the patient's consciousness can cope with it. The therapist here plays an important part in that he acts as a sort of midwife and by his presence allays the fears of the patient. We therefore have two people present at the original charging of an incident, which makes the confrontation of the unknown easier for the patient. The procedure of making known may be worrisome and frightening, but the recognition of the happenings is not.

At the same moment that an incident becomes fully known, the patient suddenly feels at ease and has no further complaints or fear. It is comparable to the birth of a child. The difficulties pertain only to the procedure itself, not to the results. It makes absolutely no difference how gruesome the experience was; once the patient is aware of it, it no longer has any effect on him.

This is an important rule: everything that is known can no longer hurt. It can happen that after obtaining conscious knowledge of an event, a person may not feel well and may suddenly feel unusually ill at ease or tense, or even have a headache. One is inclined to consider as the cause the incident that has become known and to explain the consequences as certain processing difficulties. Such an explanation is erroneous. If negative results are obtained, it means that the incident that was made known was not the actual nucleus of the complex. By uncovering an incident, however, this frees the material underlying it that now presses against the threshold of consciousness. In such a case, it is possible to continue the process rapidly since the material has risen to the surface of its own accord. Here, too, the principle is valid: symptoms and complaints are caused exclusively by unknown material, not by known matters.

When the patient relives the nuclear trauma, he relives it with all the emotions that attended it. Again the two ingredients, incident and emotion, which were separated at the time of repression, are combined. After the emotion has found its correct complementary half, however, and has again been joined with it, it no longer needs to be projected. For as mentioned at the beginning, the symptom was only the constant attempt to connect a free-flowing emotion with an incident, while the present time could only permit its projection. This procedure will suddenly collapse when the emotion has found its true place in the past; the symptom will disappear.

What we have said may temporarily suffice as a theoretical concept in order to get back to the patient to whom we introduced you at the beginning. I selected a certain symptom—her inability to leave the house alone—and had her relive this situation under hypnosis. The feeling that came to the surface, namely a very specific fear, was used as the guideline to lead us back to earlier experiences during which the same emotion appeared.

And so we quickly reached her childhood years where certain psychic connections cropped up that are familiar to every psychoanalyst: love of father, secret desire to have father as sexual partner, hatred of mother as rival, punishment of masturbation and the castration fantasy connected with this. All this is well known since the ground-breaking work of Sigmund Freud and in our case fits very well into the characteristics of our patient. I made all these associations known and produced the reference to the symptom. The internal association was understood and realized, and the symptoms began to lose some of their edge.

This procedure consumed approximately the first twenty hours of therapy. This meager amount of time used, compared to psychoanalysis, is made possible by using hypnosis. Here we combine two techniques, one being hypnosis, the other, analysis. This method, under the name of hypnoanalysis, is practiced with significantly greater frequency in the United States than in Germany.

In Germany, hypnotherapy is generally equated with suggestion therapy and is designated a "covering procedure." This form of therapy, which originated in the beginnings of hypnosis, renounces all analysis (analyze=uncover) and instead works exclusively with healing suggestions that in content are opposed to the symptoms. For example, a strong inferiority complex would be treated by repeatedly suggesting to the patient during hypnosis, "You feel at ease everywhere and all the time; you are free and self-confident!" Here one is not the least bit interested in the cause of the inferiority complex, but simply attempts to replace it with another program. The danger of this type of therapy lies on the one hand in the possibility of a relapse and on the other hand in a transference of symptoms, since the basic problem was not uncovered. In spite of this, such procedure frequently achieves convincing successes.

The ideal solution may be found in the combination of hypnoanalysis and suggestion therapy. The peculiar nature of hypnosis makes analysis considerably easier, saves time, and avoids detours, while the simultaneous positive suggestions immediately fill the newly unlocked psyche with the "desired programs." Thus it is possible, by a combination of various methods, to achieve a maximum of success, which one method alone could not do, or which at least would take considerably longer.

In Germany, we must learn to separate hypnosis therapy from classic suggestion therapy. Hypnosis alone is not a form of therapy, but a means of reaching the unconscious in a patient quickly and directly. Only when this has been accomplished does the actual therapy begin. Hypnosis only opens the door and corresponds somewhat to the surgeon's knife with which he opens the abdominal wall. Only then does the operation take place. For this reason, the fact that a therapist avails himself of hypnosis does not have the slightest bearing on his therapy.

There is no hypnosis therapy, but only therapy that uses hypnosis—which really should and could be done more frequently than it is at present. From Freud, we know how important the first years of a child's life are for later development and for the understanding of later neuroses. It is hypnosis that makes possible a particularly rapid and intensive recollection and reliving of these early years.

But at the beginning is an event that is especially important and that leaves very definite impressions, namely birth itself. The process of birth, the remarks of mother, father, doctor, and midwife made to and about the new arrival, have an effect on the baby that must not be underestimated. In the erroneous belief that the infant cannot understand a word, much is frequently said in this situation that may have a destructive effect on the newborn child. Later on, I shall go into greater detail about descriptions of the birth and what care must be taken at that time. Here we shall only call attention to the reliving of birth and the making conscious of the entire event as an important therapeutic step that should be taken in every case (but is frequently lacking!).

I shall not stop here, but go back even further in time with my patient. We look for the embryonic stage and whether the child received any impressions here that became important in its later development. With this, I refer not only to physical stimuli but to all psychic influences of the parents on the child. It is amazing to see how much damage can be done, and parents would be even more amazed if they knew how their child reacts to their behavior even in its unborn state.

The education of the child begins at the moment of conception. I make this known in my therapy. This may appear completely impossible to many and even my patients smile at me sympathetically when I offer this opinion. But everything happens much more rapidly and more easily than expected. Birth, embryo development, and conception are suddenly experienced with complete animation, optically, acoustically, and with all attending bodily sensations and pain. Here we suddenly discover the reason why all her life a woman considered herself inferior as a woman and always wanted to be a man. After conception, her father had said, "I hope we have a child, and if we do, I hope it's a boy."

In the case of our patient, which we shall continue to use as an example, the embryonic stage brought us the solution of her symptom. You may recall that she felt particular aggression toward pregnant women and considered all mothers murderers. As I pursued this symptom, I came upon an abortion attempt. The mother of my patient attempted an abortion during her third month. This powerful threat to life was the trauma we had been seeking, the one that gave the symptom its emotional stimulus. My patient experienced this abortion attempt once more with all its pain, fear, and feeling of hatred, but afterward recognized the reason for her attitude toward pregnant women and her hatred and aggression disappeared.

The analytic interpretations of other childhood experiences were not as successful. Connections were recognized and confirmed; the connection with a symptom was understood and symptoms slowly lost their edge; the patient felt better from time to time, but most of the symptoms did not disappear. The turning point came during the thirteenth session, during which Mrs. Inge S., of her own accord and without special suggestion, continued her regression and, greatly agitated, began to talk incoherently of disconnected items that did not pertain to this 28-year-old life. It was only when I realized this that I turned on the tape recorder. That is why the recording began suddenly and without introduction.

When you read such a report, you miss the drama that the session produces. The patient's entire body was agitated; she moaned and cried; then her voice would be choked and full of despair. On the occasion when she swore, she raised her clenched fist again and again. The most fascinating part, however, was an unexpected change of voice after about one-third of the session. Her normal voice suddenly became a deep, coarse voice that sounded almost like a man's. Her new voice had not the slightest resemblance to her normal voice and appeared almost ghostlike.

Added to this was the fact that this woman had not learned Latin in school and that she has no knowledge of the historical facts pertaining to ancient Rome. She knew just as little about reincarnation. She is a good Catholic, and all her symptoms were shaded in this direction. All the more surprising was the discovery that after this session the patient had no difficulties of any kind adjusting to and filing away her newly acquired experiences in a possible former life. This was verified at the end of the session, when she actually said, "I know I am becoming human, I know it; I know that this is the beginning of becoming a human being. I feel peace and happiness, oceanic, world-encompassing, no, universe-encompassing; it is such a wonderful feeling, so grand and glorious, it is not a feeling of space; it is indescribable, truly beautiful . . ."

When we met again a week later at the next therapy session, Mrs. Inge S. complained especially about a symptom that continued to disturb her. She sometimes had red marks on her face of which she was ashamed and that became particularly noticeable whenever she was about to leave the house. She was always afraid that people would be able to tell something from these marks, although she did not know what. During the course of the therapy, we had discovered that she was subconsciously afraid that people could tell from these marks that she had engaged in sexual intercourse and was ashamed of this. But even this enlightenment did not help the symptom to disappear. During the above-mentioned fourteenth session, we again began to discuss this subject as we tried to determine which symptoms had disappeared and which still remained. After the beginning of the hypnotic sleep, I made the following suggestion: "Let us go back in time until you reach the incident during which these marks first appeared." During this session, the following was recorded:

H: Who burned you?
S: That is the sun—and because I am so thirsty . . . and everyone sees me.
H: Tell me more!
S: I would like to run away—but I can't.
H: Why not?
S: Well, because—I can't—I know now—they all know something—all of them.
H: What do they know?
S: They know—they were all burned—hm—all those, with whom we were together.
H: With whom were you together?
S: Well, with the others—with—we were . . .
H: Tell me the whole story, slowly and quietly, every detail.
S: But I'm afraid—I can't!
H: What are you afraid of?
S: That is—after all, I—my parents, they are no longer there —now I know why I—because, that is why he left—that was, because we had to be baptized first, we were unable to be together then, and in the meantime the incident with my brother—and then he left.
H: What was the incident?
S: Yes, that—
H: Well, tell me.
S: I don't like to talk about that.
H: What happened?

S: When I—well, my brother—that was enough—but not because I did that, but because then he left, I got these marks—so that everyone can see that I am guilty.

H: Of what?

S: Yes, that I am guilty, and I was not baptized—because, it didn't work anymore—those are the—I don't know why I am suddenly thinking of that—with the marks, when someone commits a sin, then you are marked, and that is why we were burned.

H: Who are we?

S: I am not allowed to talk!

H: Why can't you talk?

S: Because—of my guilt—because I am always afraid—because I poisoned my brother and that is why I am afraid, and we could not get married whether—I really am not allowed to say that.

H: You may say it.

S: His name is—I can't tell you—or he will be arrested, too.

H: You need not be afraid to tell me.

S: Well, he will be baptized first—and that is what—that . . . I know the name—if I mention it—

H: What then?

S: Nothing more can happen to me—now—because he is so far away.

H: Who is he?

S: Afrahmus.

H: Afrahmus?

S: Yes.

H: Is that your friend?

S: Yes, but—why he went away—I know why.

H: Why?

S: Yes, because . . . because he knew that way he could punish me most severely—

H: Why did he want to punish you?

S: Because I—because I killed my brother and he did not like me anymore, and I was so ashamed—but I thought because I have marks now and—but he—my soul is marked; I am no longer pure, and that is why he went away, the soul—I am that—and that is why the thought of that makes me feverish—when I think that he will go away and never come back—I don't know it was —it was so far away—that is—he is there—there are hills, no, first roads, then hills, then there is the water—that is why I don't like the water, because I know he is there, and he will never come back because he is across the water—I don't know, but he is across the water and even further.

H: ——

S: Because I know that—I know that he will not come back —that is the way there—you can see that—that is where the hills are—that is the judgment place.

H: What is there?

S: That is the judgment place, where the stakes are—when you are crucified, and when you go there—it is far away—you get to a cliff—behind it is water—the sea—that is why I don't like it, and that was the sea where I always stood at the edge of the cliff, but I never really stood at the edge, I was never there—I only saw it—I never went to the precipice because I was afraid, and that's why I didn't like the water—the water, because it always reminded me—

H: Of what?

S: Well, that he went across the water, and that he is not coming back.

H: Was that your friend?

S: Yes, that was my friend.

H: Did you have an intimate relationship with him?

S: No, no, not yet—he did live with my uncle, but he—we were not even baptized—we could not marry, and it was the day of the resurrection, when it happened.

H: What happened?

S: Well, when I went into the big building and brought my brother the bread—it was as if someone tore my heart out—it was terrible . . .

H: You had no sexual relations with Afrahmus?

S: No, that would never do.

H: Why not?

S: No—we wanted to be baptized first—and I was afraid, that maybe—

H: What were you afraid of?

S: Well, it is like—not really fear, but it was simply—it just wasn't done before, that was because—of course, we were betrothed, that's why we didn't do that, and besides, it was much more beautiful—because we wanted to wait—because we knew we would get together, but then I did that and . . .

H: Now you believe you are marked?

S: Yes. [*sobs deeply*]

H: You show that externally?

S: Yes—it can be seen.

H: How?

S: My heart suddenly begins to pound and then—it can be seen—yes . . .

H: How can it be seen?

S: I don't know, hm—in my face—it can be seen, I know—it can be seen because I am going to destroy myself.

H: How?

S: Well, I want to commit suicide.

H: Why?

S: Because I want to torture myself, and I believe I must do penance.

H: How do you intend to do that?

S: I don't know myself—but it can be seen.

H: In what way?

S: Because everyone is looking at me—and everyone can see it.

H: How can they see it?

S: I don't know—I—but it's possible—no, we did not do that.

H: What?

S: I don't know—but I am not going to have a baby.

H: Then you did have sexual relations?

S: No—I don't know . . .

-77

H: Tell me more.

S: I, I don't know. I—there are two little children beside me, but they are not mine.

H: Whose are they?

S: I don't know—they just came into the building with me— I don't know why—perhaps because I have a big stomach, but—

H: Are you pregnant?

S: I don't know—I really don't know.

H: Surely you know whether you are pregnant.

S: No.

H: Could you be?

S: No—I don't know whether I could be or not—yes—but I am not pregnant—I am imagining that because I also imagine— no—it is possible.

H: What is possible?

S: That there was something.

H: Let us dissolve to that point in time . . .

S: That was it, exactly.

H: Tell me.

S: That was it, in the garden, yes—it was in the garden—but it was not allowed.

H: Tell me exactly what is happening.

S: Well, we are walking along together, and we are saying nothing—it is very pleasant, but I am still afraid.

H: Of what?

S: Well, that he wants to do that before our wedding—hm— I really love him, and since I would like it, too—now I know how it happened—because he saw us—he saw us—I don't know who he is—I know him, we all know him—and he saw it.

H: What did he see?

S: Well, he saw us making love—he saw that.

H: Where did you make love?

S: In the garden—it is really not a garden, it is—it is—there is a wall and a lawn, and there are little shrubs—it is made of wood, like an arbor, and now I'm afraid.

H: Of what?

S: Well, because we are engaged, but one must not get weak, because then you are marked—when one has done that, the others see it.

H: How do you know that?

S: Because the others say it can be seen.

H: Have you ever seen it on anyone else?

S: They have to take the veil, I don't know, the friends— they have to hide, they can't go out anymore because they can be seen.

H: Good, what else is happening in the park? There is the wall, the lawn, the little arbor . . .

S: Yes, he saw us—because he was on the terrace, and then he hid behind a pillar, and I was ashamed, terribly, really, but only, only when I saw him alone I was really ashamed. I don't know his name.

H: But you know him?

S: I don't know, I don't know his name.

H: That doesn't matter!

S: I am ashamed when I am alone with him. He saw me—and the way he looked at me—so vulgar—I turned red—there I really felt—

H: Good, let us go through this scene once more.

S: Of course, he thinks that anyone can have me, because he knows very well that we are not married; that is why I can't have a child, because, you can see that, and then, when they all look at my stomach, then they think perhaps they can have me, too —because I've done that sort of thing before—and then I get these red marks, and they won't go away, and the more I think of it, the worse it gets—and then I don't want to go out—perhaps be- cause—well, people notice it—because I prostituted myself, that was because we were not yet married, that's what I mean—and perhaps that is why he went away, and because I was guilty I get these marks in my face—and because I liked it myself—maybe —and then I was so ashamed—when I stood across the way from him, and we stood alone across from each other, and I was so ashamed—my face became so hot it felt as if someone were burning holes in my skin.

H: How do you know how it feels to have holes burned in your skin?

S: That happens—or when you feel guilty—yes—when you are supposed to talk and you don't want to talk, they burn holes in your skin.

H: Has that happened to you? Return to that incident!

S: Hm, that is the sun—I won't say anything—I know what it was—no—I was supposed to talk—but I can't—they brand you.

H: To whom were you supposed to talk?

S: They have little sponges—they burn your skin with them —sponges—they take them out of the water—and they burn them on your skin—with something sticky, it's brown—red and partly yellow when they heat it, and they dip the sponges into it, and then they press them on your skin.

H: Why do they do that?

S: So that you are marked for something.

H: Why are they doing it to you?

S: Because they believe—because I, because I, because I was seen—they think I will betray them, that I will, yes that I will betray Christ—hm, they say I have betrayed Him—because I prostituted myself—hm—and those are our friends in the house, but he is an evil person—yes—that was—he was the one who told me to murder my brother—Tau . . .

H: Let us return to your burning face and to these sponges —tell me how this is done—tell me exactly what is happening— tell me everything you feel—what is going on—who is there— what are they saying?

S: It is a room—a room—a long table or a bench—a long bench and there are long—hm—they spear the sponges and dip them in this liquid—hm—I'm afraid of it—they dip them in this liquid and then they press them on our skin.

H: Our skin? Who are we?

S: Well, there are three other women and they have been

accused, too—but not like me—and with these sponges they wanted to—

H: Do they want you to confess or to talk?

S: Yes they want me to talk.

H: What do they want you to say?

S: Hm, that I defiled the church—this is in my uncle's house—

H: What is in your uncle's house? Where this is happening?

S: Yes.

H: Who is present?

S: There are—I don't know, but there are only—five men, I think—no—yes—and one is especially cruel.

H: Why, what is he doing?

S: He is pressing the little sponge on my skin—he's the one—yes, he is hunchbacked and small.

H: What is he?

S: Hunchbacked and small—and I'm afraid—really.

H: How big are the little sponges?

S: As big as—as big as the—not round like these—hm, one might say as big as [*heavy breathing*] . . .

H: As big as the end of your thumb?

S: Like four small thumb-ends, four little fingernails.

H: Like four fingernails? Good, then let us fade back to the moment when they were placed on your face.

S: But it must not hurt—I'm so afraid and I will not admit anything . . .

H: What is happening? Tell me every detail.

S: There is a rail and there are many—such—

H: What?

S: Such—what you pierce the sponges with—they are lying ready because you pick up the sponges with them—otherwise he might burn himself; he puts the sponges on them and then he turns them in his vessel—and it hangs on a—there is a fire under it—and that is in the wall, and he dips it into the hot liquid, and it is so hot it makes everything stick, and then he presses it on your face.

H: Where is he pressing one now?

S: Well, he is pressing it—he is pressing it on my face, and it burns like fire—he is putting it on my face just where everyone can see it, then—all over and from the side, and I am getting so hot—[*sobs*]

H: Good, how many has he put on you?

S: I don't know.

H: Well, count them.

S: He put one here, then he is pressing one here . . .

H: Tell me more.

S: Then he is burning my chin, and especially hard on my cheeks.

H: Where else?

S: On my neck.

H: Not on your forehead?

S: Yes, ah, but it is so hot—I am getting all—he wanted to—that is why my eyes are burning so—because he—it hurts . . .

H: Keep talking.

S: He has disfigured my whole face—he is burning me fiercely—he is burning me terribly—I can't touch it at all—it burns even more.

H: What else is happening?

S: I don't feel it anymore, but he is starting in again, and there is an old man.

H: What is there?

S: And therefore—so that he will stop—and this cruel individual—he is burning my face again—deeply—so that it can be seen—I am so hot . . .

H: What else is going on?

S: I don't know—he—something is pulling on my legs—because, he is still pulling.

H: What is he doing?

S: He is pulling on my legs—I—that hurts—he is pulling so hard.

H: How is he doing that—how is he pulling?

S: There—with such—it is a wheel—he is pulling my foot apart—that is the wheel—it hurts so much.

H: Why is he doing this to you?

S: So that I will repent.

H: What are you supposed to repent?

S: That I did that.

H: Did what?

S: Because I was with—because I was with Afrahmus in the garden—because, because we made love there—before we were married and before the baptism—and . . .

H: What is happening now?

S: He is burning my face—hm—he is burning my face—hm. [*cries and sobs*]

H: What else is happening?

S: He is still pulling, pulling on my legs—he wants to tear my legs out—he is pulling my leg apart—it is getting all—stiff, I don't know.

H: Continue.

S: I don't know—I think I am getting sick . . .

H: Continue. Tell me what else is happening!

S: There is a room—and they are laying me down—on a blanket on the floor—yes—and then there is a woman, she has cloths, and she is putting the cloths around my head—and she is putting something inside the clothes, something green and transparent—and then—I feel such pain—because he—my leg—but I need not be afraid that I will be tortured like that again.

H: Why?

S: Because I am already marked—hm—so everyone can see—I can't go over all that again—it is too much—I can't look over it all.

H: What can't you look over?

S: Because it is too much.

H: What is too much? What is too much?

S: Because I am all confused—I didn't know that something, hm—because it was so beautiful and not bad, I knew I must not do it, but, hm—I didn't know they would punish me so severely, I didn't know that—but I know I will never do it again—never again—I don't want to see it anymore, either—because he—because the way he looked at me—no one helped me say anything —hm.

H: Good. Let us leave this incident, but before we do, can you tell me what year this is?

S: I—I know—it is 3—I only see—I . . .

H: What do you see?

S: That is 3—I am afraid of that number.

H: Why, how does it look?

S: Because I—see the—that is the number—that is in the wall of the building, but because I cannot read—not really . . .

H: Tell me how the number looks.

S: Hm, I would like to say—I don't know, whether that is right or whether we—whether we say that today, I can't read it—but I know that it's called—that is—can I say that—I don't know.

H: What do you mean?

S: Well, I can't read it, but I know that it's called—well, I mean, if I, the way it is today, I can read it—but I can't say it.

H: Describe it.

S: It is with an M—always with an M.

H: With an M and then?

S: Yes, and then a [*makes signs in the air with her hand*]. And that is like that.

H: A V.

S: Yes, MXM.

H: MXM.

S: Yes, MXM, I don't know—and then it's like—that is nothing, and then there is 1, 2, 3, 4, and a V, I don't know, that is . . .

H: Good, let us leave this number; we shall leave this time period, leave these events, and go forward in time. Your face is clean, completely clear and spotless. Your skin is clean and smooth. You can feel the marks dissolve, isn't that right?

S: Yes, they are disappearing!

H: Because they have no further justification.

S: True, they don't.

H: You don't need them anymore. You don't want them anymore. We shall simply let them disappear—very simple—these marks have made an error in time—they are two thousand years too late. All your fears, all your feelings of guilt are errors in time. We don't need them anymore. You are now living in the year 1975. Guilt feelings from the past are no longer valid—how do you feel?

S: Very well.

H: Then we shall end this session promptly.

Here we have reached the most decisive point of my therapeutic method. I claim—and this claim can be proved easily by any expert—that one comes almost automatically upon earlier incarnations if only one searches persistently enough for the actual cause of a symptom. My experiences indicate that the great majority of all symptoms have their origins in earlier incarnations and not in this life. Everything we usually describe as the cause of a symptom is not the real cause but only a larger or smaller link in the chain that would eventually lead us to the cause.

In the psychotherapy commonly practiced up to this time, one would unwind the thread and follow it to a childhood experience, designate this as the cause, and thus heal the symptom. This procedure works in so many cases because by using it, a mass of psychic energy (charge) is built up. This in turn leads to a noticeable alleviation of the patient's problems, which can then be brought to a healing stage by suggesting that the true cause has been discovered. All this, however, does not tell us whether or not the actual cause has been found.

I claim that previously it was a rare case that anyone came in contact with the actual traumata. The fault lies with the axiomatic prejudice of our Western world, which without exception wants to understand this life as an existence that flashes just once upon this earth. One can, however, only perceive as much of actuality as one considers theoretically and basically possible. As long as man considered a flight to the moon basically impossible, he could never land on this satellite. It is the same with reincarnation. As long as I am firm as a rock in my conviction that there is no previous existence, I shall, of course, never find one. It is no wonder, therefore, that formerly all analysis was discontinued when approaching the time of birth, instead of continuing until nothing further was developed.

Let it be noted that a former life need not at all be suggested to a patient in order to discover it. The patient will not reward the expectations of a reincarnation-hungry therapist with beautiful stories, but rather it will be found that former experiences of the patient will rise to the surface of their own accord if he is simply ordered to return to the true cause of his symptom or emotion. One condition for this, of course, is that the patient must not let everything that he talks about and reports drip continually through his rational filter, but must passively yield himself to whatever happens to him. Conscious controls and the attempt by the patient to fit everything into its proper place and analyze it will keep the unknown material from rising to the surface. In stages of deep hypnosis, there is usually no control of the rational, which is why hypnosis makes our procedure considerably easier. In any case, it is by no means necessary. Patients difficult to hypnotize can, by practice with the symbol drama, be taught to report, without interference on their part, pictures and experiences that come to the surface on their own. Later, I shall discuss the technique in detail. Here it is important to make certain that events outside this current life not be in any way suggested but be permitted to appear as a perfectly natural happening by giving the patient the opportunity to see them that way.

Strange to say, up to now it was usually considered neither necessary nor even possible to investigate the embryonic period. The interesting and important events that are to be found here can be seen, in addition to the above-mentioned abortion trauma, from the following example of another patient.

Miss A., thirty-two years old, experienced her embryonic stage during her sixteenth therapy session. Her mother is in her seventh month and learns from the doctor that she is going to have twins. My patient is greatly agitated. "My mother doesn't want me—but I am here! She doesn't want any child at all and instead, there are two of us—and she doesn't want two, either!" Miss A. cries. "My mother is desperate because there are two— I could scream!" She cries.

"Mommy, I am here. I am here whether you want me or not!" She pounds with her fists. "I am angry. I am very angry. Mommy, I could kill you—you don't love me, but I need you, I hate you!" She cries. "I don't want to eat anymore; I want nothing more from you."

I ask her, "Why?"

Miss A.: "Because she doesn't want me either. My sister can have everything—I want nothing more!" With these words, she cringes, turns on her side, and presses her face tightly against the couch. "I want to die—I've had enough—my sister is taking up all the room, damn it!" After some silence, she resumes, "I must be born—I want to live—I must—I will—I'm going to make it. I don't want to die. I want to, I must live!" The biography of Miss A. confirms: she was born after her sister, and while her twin sister was strong and healthy, Miss A. had to be taken to a clinic immediately. She was very tiny and barely able to live. She remained in an incubator for six weeks, and no one believed she would survive.

We see how early in life psychic events can begin and what effect they can have on a person. The fact that in school psychology an embryo is not believed capable of the psychic reaction to the extent described above again reflects the axiom that consciousness and thinking are products of material discharges. People nowadays have such a fixation with this pattern that they cannot even hypothetically turn around the point of reference and determine whether it would not be more logical and more productive to consider the psychic process as the primary one and the material happening as a product of consciousness. If matter could create consciousness, it should not be too difficult to create human beings artificially. But it is on this reef that even the most sagacious experiments run aground. They will continue to run aground as long as it is not recognized that the psychic concept of consciousness is required before matter can be made to live.

Psychopharmacotherapy falls prey to the same error. It too attempts to interfere with material events and bring about changes. But the cause of all behavior and misbehavior lies with the psyche, which is not matter. This is the source of all items of information, which are converted into action by the body. In this close contact between psyche and the body, every bit of interference brings about a change. For this reason, the effectiveness of psychopharmacology is not an argument for the correctness of this procedure. If one wishes to heal, changes should be made in the primary system, namely, in the psyche.

For the understanding of my therapeutic procedure, it is important to assign consciousness an independent existence that is not first created by the body, because when I have passed through the embryo stage to the time of conception with my patients, we proceed further back in time, even though during the period preceding conception we no longer have a body. In spite of this, everyone can find himself existing as the "ego" without being able to determine time, space, or location. If my patients go back still further, they will come upon another physical existence, but will continue to retain the same "ego" as before. There is no break in the continuity. The custom of identifying one's "ego" with one's body suddenly disappears during the session. The body is found to be something that can be put on and taken off at will, just as we are always the same human being, whether we wear clothing or not and regardless of what clothing we are wearing.

This unbroken continuity of the human psyche that goes beyond individual incarnations makes it possible to understand why symptoms in the current life may have their origins as far back as hundreds of years ago. Just as today's experience will maintain its reality tomorrow, even though a whole night may intervene, so the events of the last several thousand years continue to affect us. The sum of all incarnations forms our learning history. This learning history of ours makes us whatever we happen to be and stamps our conduct and emotions. The learning history since our last birth, however, does not alone make us what we are today.

Interesting, but probably surprising, after what we have said above, is the fact that the psychic material of earlier incarnations is subject to the same psychological laws that we find in psychoanalysis. This brings us to an important practical problem. When we transport a subject or a patient back into an earlier life, it is only rarely that at the beginning we get a report of his earlier life that corresponds in every detail to his actual historical experience. The story will be falsified by the same psychic mechanisms that falsify any other report he might give us, such as that of his current childhood or similar experiences, because those facts that have too high an emotional charge cannot be confronted at first. In order to conceal the repressed material, dates are changed and transposed. If during further sessions a trauma is found and made known, this will generally create a new arrangement of certain previously stated facts. An example may illustrate this.

For several sessions, a subject spoke about having been a teacher and having had to leave the place of her activity during a certain year because the school was suddenly closed. When she was asked about the reason for the closing of the school, she gave a vague answer. Only during a later session did I learn that during this year she was expecting a child by her lover and finally had it aborted. This abortion experience was highly charged with energy and for that reason was at first suppressed. When this incident became known, however, she also confessed that her pregnancy was the reason that she had left school and that the closing of the school was simply a subterfuge.

Many sessions later, I chanced upon another serious trauma. The subject had fallen down the steps at the age of four in an earlier life and had broken a leg. Because of a complication or possible malpractice, the leg remained crippled and for the rest of her life she could not walk properly. It took me almost an hour to make this crippled leg known and to decrease the charge step by step until the patient was in a condition to completely accept reality.

At the same time, this caused a change in several other factors. She had actually never been a teacher but had all her life wanted to be one. Her problems and the occasional use of a wheelchair prevented her from realizing this profession. Instead, she helped out temporarily in a school and earned a living teaching remedial classes from time to time. All these details had to be reshaped, however, as long as the underlying trauma, the injured leg, was not yet known.

I hope that this example will make clear how in a previous life we frequently become victims of repression and defensive measures and cover recollections to an even greater extent than in the analysis of our current life. The subjects, however, do not say something new or different every time. The same statements are made each time even if one allows the first reports to be forgotten and thereby eliminates the possibility of a reproduction of recollections. The change of facts only begins when a previously unrecognized trauma becomes known. All the items that were necessary to veil this trauma then suddenly disappear and the details reshape themselves.

Therapeutically this process is very interesting and lends considerable support to the theory of reincarnation. After all, the fact that the recollected material of earlier incarnations must conform to the same laws as the recollections of the current life clearly indicates that we are dealing with remembrances of earlier days. It is extremely unlikely that material that has been read, heard, or discovered serves as a basis for the laws of suppression.

In addition to concealing deeply ingrained traumata, the patient has another method of approaching unpleasant situations step by step without confronting them all at once. Here the patient experiences situations that represent the theme of the trauma in an excessive or greatly changed form, without ever having actually experienced such situations. These are fantasies that are related thematically to an as yet undiscovered trauma.

This has a certain resemblance to a dream in which similar instances may occur.

With regard to the historical verification of earlier lives, these fantasies and suppressions represent a great source of error and a considerable disturbance factor, but not in therapeutic activity. For by living through these fantasies, the patient gradually helps to reduce the charge in his suppressed complexes, which helps us to get continually closer to the real situation until it is suddenly clearly recognized. Fortunately the fantasy experiences usually distinguish themselves so clearly from real recollections that they can be differentiated with considerable accuracy.

This is not particularly important for the therapeutic process, since the first thing to consider is the gradual discharge of energy and since with time the patient will come upon the actual events by himself. Characteristic of the fantasies is first of all a quality of unreality in the patient's description of them, since, like a dream, fantasies have no regard for logic and reality. Added to this is the evidence that a fantasy experience cannot be continued on both sides of a time coordinate. By this, I mean that during the description of experiences in incarnation, I can jump back and forth in time simply by asking, "Where were you a year before this incident?" or "What will happen now?" This continuity of reporting does not work with fantasy experiences. In such instances, an event is described that stands alone in space and has no relation to either past or future. The last and safest method of differentiation is the repetition of events in various sessions. The fantasy experiences change shape almost every time, since the level of energy is different on each occasion.

Reports regarding incarnations never change when they are true. Many individuals, in their waking state after a session, can sense which of their stories were real and which were not quite accurate. This is the above-mentioned ability to differentiate between dreams and reality. Dreams or fantasies only create a feeling of identity as long as one is dreaming. In a waking condition, the fact that it was a dream is immediately recognized.

The manner of reporting is usually equally distinct. While fantasies may be reported quite dramatically, they generally lack clear and detailed explanations. Questions about details are either avoided or answered nebulously. It is considerably different with actual recollections. Their almost every detail can be answered with great accuracy.

It is the methodical procedure that determines whether one obtains more recollections or fantasies. Basically, there are two ways of probing the past:

1. It is suggested to the subject that he go back further and further in time. For example: "We are going back in time. The past will become the present. You are getting younger. You are twenty years old, ten years old, five years old. Let us dissolve to the time of your birth. You are being born. We are now five months before your birth. We are proceeding further back to the time of conception. You will continue to go back further in time until a new situation develops. There you will stop and tell me about it!"

2. A particular feeling or emotion is selected from this life and is followed further and further back into the past. Let us take, for example, the fear of people. We begin by letting the patient relive and relate any experience in which the fear of people was present. Then we go back further in time and let him report another incident concerning fear of people. Thus the patient, on his own, reaches even earlier years, does not stop with his birth, but continues constantly to go back further in time. New experiences will begin to surface on their own, experiences that are from a completely different chronological era.

With method 1, we always reach an old life almost immediately, which, however, at first need not agree in every detail with historic reality, yet, as a whole, encompasses an incarnation. The reverse is usually the case with method 2. Since in this instance we are pursuing an emotion, a trauma is usually approached automatically so that there is a much greater likelihood of receiving a series of fantasies that help pave the way energetically to the actual incident. If we are looking for incarnations, method 1 leads us to our goal more quickly and more surely. For therapeutic purposes, method 2 is frequently indicated because it generally leads to the trauma we seek without digressing to any great extent. In therapy, only the traumatic events interest us, and it is not necessary to completely review every life from the cradle to the grave.

In order to classify the above-mentioned possibilities conceptually, I shall speak of three different levels from which the information in a therapy session can derive.

The first level is the symbol drama, with reference to the terminology of Professor Leuner (also called catathymic picture life).

The second level I call the psychodrama. In this case, problems and conflicts are projected by a method not previously known onto a new time period and reported as experiences.

The third level is the reality level. Here we are dealing with actual recollections from earlier incarnations.

Starting with the level of the psychodrama, we find something completely new, something that was not previously known in psychotherapy. By suggestively moving the time period, I give the patient the opportunity to project unconscious problems and conflict material closer to reality than was previously possible. What happens on an experimental basis is similar to what previously was possible only for poets and authors, namely, the transposition of autobiographical data into a bygone era. The patient in a psychodrama can play himself with unbelievable exactness and at the same time experience himself without requiring a symbol.

Many of you may be inclined to explain as psychodrama what I designate as reincarnation recollection. Even if this were the case, the therapeutic procedure of regression into the past would no doubt be a new and most effective instrument of psychotherapy, since the effectiveness of reincarnation therapy remains unaffected, whether we are dealing with a historic life or a projection. In spite of this, I consider the interpretation of a reincarnation description as a psychodrama untenable. Psychodrama can originate only with the projection of problems, be they conscious or unconscious. This would in no way explain the following phenomena:

Subjects have described historical incidents with amazing accuracy and exactness. For example, one subject, a radio reporter in this life and a dry goods dealer in the year 1755 in his previous life, measured the material for a suit in ells, counted money in thalers, and talked about a hunger catastrophe in the year 1732 which event was later verified in a chronicle.

Another subject in talking about a previous life spoke almost exclusively about measures, numbers, and distances. He was a builder at that time. He described the smallest details in buildings that had been constructed under his supervision and only much later began to talk about personal matters. His occupation completely dominated the conversation. In this case, it is questionable how far we can go in translating these descriptions into projections of present-day problems. If one goes through several lives with a subject, individual incarnations are often so different that they could by no means be the product of a projection from the one current life.

A twenty-year-old female student, for example, spoke in great detail about an abortion in a previous life. It was proved that in this life she had never had to deal with the problems of pregnancy or abortion. The same subject experienced change of life during her sessions. She later described as a most unusual experience the fact that as a twenty-year-old she had gone through menopause. According to her own statements, this helped her understand her mother considerably better than before.

The descriptions of earlier lives are not simply conglomerations of problems, conflicts, and cliché performances, but contain so many impersonal time-specific statements and acts that the pattern of a psychodrama just does not suffice as an explanation. Subjects have told us exactly in what time they covered which distance with a coach, how bread was baked in the eighteenth century, and how in 1687 wounds were healed with certain herbs. I have conducted many experiments with young, unmarried girls who spoke of their marital problems in an earlier life. I should also like you to recall previously mentioned phenomena such as scars, temple dances, foreign languages, changes in handwriting, and so forth.

All these are reasons why I also differentiate between the level of psychodrama and the reality level. Here we find the recollection of an earlier life that by no means arises out of fantasy. At worst, a few matters in that life might be falsified in order to hide certain suppressed incidents. The same can be said with regard to recollections from this life. In order to obtain an earlier life in its purest form, without falsifications or adulterants, we must pass through the same life repeatedly during our sessions. Errors that persist will eventually be unmasked of their own accord.

This procedure may be very time-consuming and is only worthwhile if one intends to perform historical research. This historical research is more difficult than expected, the reason being that for verification we can only use specific names and dates. These, however, are matters that are of least importance to subjects. The numbers of the years and the names of towns or streets create no emotional charges in humans, so that they are very difficult to remember.

This is even easier to understand when we consider conditions in days gone by. If it is difficult today for most people to try to furnish the exact date of an event that happened several years ago, how much more difficult must it have been for someone in the seventeenth century who had never left his home town to furnish accurate information concerning locations or references to dates. To remember something, one needs some emotional charge. We all know that from our own experiences. How do you recall what you had for dinner just a month ago today? You can probably remember, however, what you had for dinner on your wedding day, twenty years ago. Here the event has a personal reference and is emotionally charged. Thus the above-mentioned reporter and former dry goods dealer was able to furnish detailed information concerning his business such as accurate measures and correct prices, but could not give us the exact name of his home town.

A third possible source of error has also crystallized. There is the possibility that at the beginning several lives overlapped. This occurs especially when two or more previous lives have common points of contact such as identical towns, similar occurrences, and so on. The same thing happens to someone who wants to reconstruct a specific birthday or Christmas celebration. At first the events of several birthdays may overlap, and one has to go through a sorting-out process to determine where everything belongs. We have experienced the same thing in some of our sessions. The sorting-out becomes easier by virtue of the fact that more lives reach the conscious stage. The proper sorting-out then presents scarcely any difficulties.

All these are possible sources of error that must be recognized and considered. Sometimes several errors will occur at the same time; sometimes the life is so vividly described that it never again changes. From a therapeutic point of view, all this plays a subordinate role. It is sufficient to be aware of the sources of error so that specific developments can be understood.

Before I explain the technical phase of reincarnation therapy systematically once more, I should like to present another typical report of therapy that describes the trauma of a patient with a fear. She is twenty-two years old and married. This report is the result of following the feeling of fear further and further back in time (regression method 2). By the nature of the statements made, we recognize the high charge and feel the conflict between the desire not to see the suppressed incident and my pressure on the subject to confront it now.

H: Continue.

S: What am I to do? I can't defend myself against all these people.

H: What is happening?

S: They are cutting off my hair—they are laughing about it. Funny, I think—they seem to think it's a good idea—I am being punished.

H: What else is happening?

S: I don't know—I don't know—do they do things like that?

H: What are they doing?

S: They are putting a heavy rope around me—they are ridiculing me—laughing at me—I don't like the way they are laughing at me.

H: Who is putting the rope around you?

S: One of the people.

H: Who is it?

S: I don't know—don't know him.

H: Do you recognize him?

S: Only from having seen him.

H: How old are you, anyway?

S: Forty, fifty.

H: Exactly!

S: The people are all of different ages.

H: How old are you?

S: Twenty.

H: Exactly twenty?

S: Yes.

H: What else is happening? You have a rope around your neck. Do you feel it?

S: Actually I feel nothing—I don't feel like—they are all pressing—maybe only symbolic—there . . .

H: What else is happening?

S: Someone is standing behind me—he is acting as if he wants to hang me—hang me.

H: But he is only pretending?

S: He is only pretending—it's terrible!

H: How is he doing that?

S: He lifts up the end of the rope and acts as if he wants to strangle me!

H: As if . . . ?

S: As if he wants to strangle me.

H: What else is happening? Look at it closely.

S: I don't know—please, please don't—but standing there so long—ridiculed by the people, abused by them—and then they send me away again—you know—it wouldn't have been so bad if they had hanged me—something like this is much worse— you always carry it with you—you never forget it—never, never . . .

H: Let's go back once more—they are putting a rope around your neck and are pretending they want to hang you.

S: Yes.

H: Then what happens?

S: The people are shouting—why doesn't he hang me—but it's not being done—he's not doing it—no—I'm supposed to suffer the punishment all my life—

H: What punishment?

S: What the people did to me!

H: All right, how does it go on? Are they putting the rope around your neck again? Tell me exactly!

S: You know, he is saying, he wants me to go away, then somehow he is hitting me.

H: How?

S: He is hitting me—the man.

H: But how?

S: Yes—I can't say it—

H: Where is he hitting you?

S: He wants me to fall down—I'm almost falling—it's on my back—he wants me to go ahead, and the people are making a path for me, standing on both sides, insulting me—and I'm supposed to go through there——

H: You are going through! Tell me everything exactly!

S: Yes.

H: And the man is following you?

S: No, he is standing still now.

H: I thought he was beating you.

S: Yes.

H: How is he doing that?

S: I don't know how to explain it.

H: Does he have something in his hand?

S: No, he is hitting me with his hands—forcing me in the direction of where the people are—where he wants me to go—I'm almost falling down—then I'm supposed to run further—further away . . .

H: Very well, what are you doing next? Where are you looking?

S: At the people.

H: What do you see?

S: The faces of the people—terrible—don't understand it—don't know why these people want to ruin my whole life.

H: Tell me more!

S: And the lines are very long—I'm supposed to go through them.

H: This place is in front of the church?

S: Yes.

H: Is today Sunday?

S: Not Sunday—a Catholic day, but not Sunday.

H: What sort of day is today?

S: A Catholic day—they are celebrating something—I don't know—something to do with mother—some sort of holiday—I don't know what—a holiday—the mother of God is being honored—I don't know what it's called—

H: What time of year is it?

S: I think it's spring.

H: What year is this?

S: 1496.

H: What month is it?

S: May.

H: What day in May?

S: May 19—they are honoring Mary.

H: Very well, let us return to the beginning of this incident. How did you get to this place? Go back to the beginning—let's relive the entire happening with all details and specifics—

you will relive everything once more. How did you get to this place?

S: You know—it's a holiday—you're supposed to go to church.

H: Are you going to church?

S: Yes—today in the month of May—we honor Mary—yes—I wanted to go there, too.

H: What are you wearing?

S: A dress.

H: How does it look?

S: Not very pretty—just plain.

H: What color?

S: It is checked, with various colors, yes, checked, but only dark colors—such as brown and dark blue.

H: How does the dress look?

S: I think it's a little too big for me—old colors—a few buttons in front—coarse—like a sack—very plain.

H: How long is your dress?

S: It covers my knees.

H: Very well, you are going to church—in what town are you?

S: I don't know—a very small town.

H: What is the name of the town—in what country are you?

S: In southern France—it looks like southern Belgium—I don't know—they look alike.

H: Is it France or Belgium? What's the name of the town?

S: Beaufort or something like that.

H: So today is a holiday and you intend to go to church!

S: Yes—May 19.

H: Are you going alone? Without your family?

S: Yes.

H: What happens next?

S: I am going to church, and as always, the people are gathering in front of the church, standing there and talking to one another—and when I arrived—the talking stopped—suddenly—something was wrong—something was wrong.

H: What do you feel? What do you hear?

S: The people stop talking—then—then they walk toward the church—then they are walking toward me, somehow they are surrounding me, I don't know what that's supposed to mean—

H: What are you doing now?

S: I am standing there.

H: Where?

S: At the place—and there are people around me—they are looking at me—mocking me—

H: And what are you doing?

S: I don't know—just standing there—amazed—I don't know what's the matter—what is happening.

H: What do you think?

S: I don't know—perhaps I did something. Can't think of anything bad—I broke a law.

H: What sort of law?

S: They must have always followed me—when we thought that no one was there—

H: Who are we?

S: The man and I.

H: Who was the man?

S: I loved him.

H: Don't you love him anymore?

S: I did love him!

H: You said "loved"!

S: Yes, in the woods—we made love in the woods, you know, but he was married—he was married—but we loved each other— we always thought we were alone—you know, he felt I was unhappy, always alone—and he wanted to make me happy—what's wrong with that?

H: Do you think that this is why the people are standing around you?

S: Yes.

H: What happens next? The people are standing around you— you have this feeling—what is happening?

S: They are starting to call me names!

H: What is the first thing you hear?

S: Whore—and now I know I was right—that I was never there alone—then I knew, yes—then I knew—

H: What happens next?

S: You know, they said I was bad!

H: Relive it now.

S: I don't know—I feel uneasy—something is going to happen.

H: What is happening?

S: They are calling me names—they say I am a whore—I am just standing there—I am stupid, too.

H: Where are you looking?

S: At the floor—but that way, by looking down at the floor, and not at the people—I am admitting some guilt—as if I were really guilty.

H: Do you have a guilty conscience?

S: Somehow, yes, I guess so—although I was very happy, somehow I had feelings of guilt.

H: What happens next? The people are calling you names!

S: Yes—I'm afraid—don't know what they will do—can't defend myself—they are punishing me for my shameful deed.

H: How are they doing that?

S: They are pulling my hair and my clothes.

H: What kind of hair do you have?

S: Long hair.

H: What color?

S: Dark.

H: The people are pulling at it?

S: Yes, and mocking me . . .

H: What happens next?

S: They are calling me names—"You fool"—my dress is coming off—I am so ashamed—I don't like that.

H: They tore off your clothes?

S: Yes.

H: How are you standing there now?

S: Half-naked.

H: What are you wearing?

S: Sort of—something like a shirt—a dress like a shirt—and shoes.

H: Take a good look at yourself—the way you are standing there now.

S: A shirt like . . .

H: What sort of feeling do you have now?

S: Terrible—when you stand there like that—you don't feel like a human being—the people shouting—calling out—and I was standing there in the woods like that, and it didn't matter to me—that's something entirely different—it was entirely different—I am so ashamed—and then comes the man with the rope, because someone called out that they ought to hang me. Now he's putting the rope around my neck—the people are laughing and applauding.

H: What is your feeling now?

S: That I am ashamed—I would like to be far away—all the people standing there—are watching—they are always making comparisons.

H: What sort of comparisons?

S: I didn't live the way I should have, you know. Today is a holiday—for Mary, the mother of God—Mary—Mary, that was a woman—that is the way one should live—that is the way to be—and then, you know, what I did, that isn't right—it's a terrible shame . . .

H: What is the man with the rope doing now?

S: You know, he is pretending that he intends to hang me—he does that just to mock me—of course, the people think that's wonderful.

H: What are your feelings?

S: You know, being dead isn't so bad—better than standing there in shame—standing there in front of those people—it's terrible—you feel like nothing—you feel like nothing—

H: What happens now?

S: Well, I've been standing there long enough—now I'm supposed to go and live with my shame—live like that forever—then

I'm to go past those people—then they will make a path for me—and I'm to go through it—

H: How does that feel?

S: Terrible—I am so ashamed—I'm not like a human being anymore . . .

H: Will they do anything to you when you go through?

S: No—no—they are pulling on my shirt—they are calling me names until I no longer hear them—until I am gone . . .

H: Where will you go? What will you do then?

S: Someone threw my dress after me—threw it at me—and I just ran—ran away—away from those people.

H: Where to?

S: Somewhere near the water—there was water—I sat down there—I'm at the edge of the water—a little lake.

H: What are you doing now?

S: I am still crying!

H: You are crying?

S: Yes—I think now I will have to live with my shame all my life—always be ashamed—always be ashamed—I can't look them in the eye anymore—can't look them in the eye—

H: You've decided to be ashamed all your life?

S: Yes.

H: Always to be ashamed and never look anyone in the eye again?

S: Yes.

H: What else are you thinking about?

S: For me, there will never be love—never—never! I will always be ashamed—something sordid will always be attached to my body—will always cling to me.

H: What happens next? How long will you sit by the water?

S: For a long time—until it is dark—then I am going home.

H: What will happen then?

S: I am going home, and then I will go to my room. My father knew it all—he already had someone in mind who was to marry me—no one wanted to marry me now, but he knew someone and I was to marry him.

H: Have we overlooked an important detail of this story—have we overlooked something that is important to this event?

S: The fact that the people tore the clothing from my body—you know—I thought that was terrible.

H: You stood there in your shirt?

S: Yes.

H: Did anything else happen, other than what you have just told me?

S: No, but I thought it was a terrible shame.

H: Did they tear off even more?

S: No, I think I was standing among those people naked.

H: They tore off all your clothing?

S: Yes.

H: You were completely naked?

S: Yes.

H: Look at the scene clearly!

S: Yes, I had only a small chain—something small hanging on it—a little heart was attached to it, a heart—that I had gotten as a gift—nothing else.

H: They undressed you completely?

S: Yes.

H: Let us dissolve to this point once more.

S: I don't like that—I can't defend myself—I was supposed to stand there as I had stood in the woods—they say it means nothing to me—but it does—I am ashamed.

H: Tell us again how you are being undressed. Who is doing it?

S: That fellow standing behind me.

H: What is he doing?

S: Tearing off my dress—you know, the dresses I wore were always so big. I want to hold the dress together—but he tears it out of my hand—tears everything to pieces—my shirt—I'm completely naked now—completely naked.

H: What else is going on?

S: Nothing—just that they are calling me names—and there is someone else there I know.

H: Who is that?

S: The man who made love to me.

H: What is he doing?

S: Just looking—looking at me—looking.

H: How do you feel about this?

S: Terrible—now he's just like the others—terrible, terrible— you know, when I was alone with him, it didn't matter—he saw me naked then—but now—now—

H: How do you feel when you see him? How is he looking at you?

S: He's not angry—no, not that—but such an empty stare— no love—no hatred—I still love him—I know we will never see each other again, never again, never.

H: Very well, let us leave this incident and go forward in time, always forward until we reach the year 1975. We shall stop on June 4, 1975.

THE METHOD OF REINCARNATION THERAPY

The following brief description of the technical aspect of reincarnation therapy is intended primarily for the professionally interested reader. Most certainly, it is not intended as directions for use and to encourage the layman to attempt these experiments. I specifically wish to warn against eliciting previous lives from one another out of curiosity or to pass the time. This method involves a deep invasion of the human psyche that should be restricted exclusively to therapy or to especially esoteric training. Playing games may result in unpleasant surprises. This does not mean that this method is particularly dangerous, but even a bread knife can cause great damage in the hands of children. It depends entirely on how well the user can handle it.

The reader trained in psychology will have no difficulty obtaining a clear picture of the method from the following outline. It is also left up to him to decide whether and to what extent he wishes to use this technique. Those seriously interested (by this I mean physicians, psychotherapists, and other practitioners of the art of healing) are nevertheless urged to learn the method personally in courses, since in the meantime a large number of new techniques have been developed that considerably facilitate its execution in daily practice, but are extremely difficult to describe in writing.

Reincarnation therapy is divided into various phases that I shall now describe step by step.

1. The Diagnosis

In this therapy, this factor is not very important at the start. After a physician's examination has assured us that an organic disorder (such as a brain tumor, etc.) is not the primary cause of a symptom, we are satisfied with an exact description of the symptomatology, its beginning, and the factors that release it. Depending on the patient, this can be done in three sentences or it may require an entire biography. It is not necessary at this stage to enter into major speculation regarding possible psychic connections. One should especially avoid attempting to classify each patient or his symptom too rapidly. What his problem may be is completely unimportant at this time; what is important is that he is here and needs help. The longer it takes to understand a patient, the better the chance that eventually we will understand him correctly. To force a case into some sort of classification during the very first hour is in most instances clearly doing the patient an injustice.

At the start of a therapeutic treatment, the patient and the therapist must join to begin the voyage into the soul together. Neither one knows from the start what the trip will be like, what experiences await them, and where it will lead. Joining together with the therapist strengthens the patient for his journey. But even if the therapist accompanies the patient as helper and advisor, it still remains a trip through the realm of the patient's soul. For this reason, I generally find an opportunity during the first session to tell the patient that everything that happens in therapy must be done by him and that I can do absolutely nothing for him. I shall simply try to be a good companion and guide.

Healing is our goal, and I mean this literally. Healing means to recover, to get better; to approach recovery is development. Only the patient himself can bring about development; no matter what, this task cannot be turned over to the therapist. Such discussion is often necessary at the beginning of therapy in order to draw the patient out of the passive state that he brings with him from his usual visits to the doctor: "I hope the doctor can give me an injection to make me well again!" To wait for a therapist to do something can bring the entire therapy to a standstill. Once the patient understands his task, he begins to enjoy participating actively in his development. This attitude toward therapy should clearly indicate that greater expenditure of diagnostic time is unnecessary.

To me, the most important source of information for a diagnosis is a horoscope. A horoscope can indicate the fundamental structure and problems of the patient and supply us with information about the basic problems which brought the patient to the present situation. A horoscope is without doubt the most individual and most exact method of diagnosis because it is the personal reproduction of this one human being without using statistical standardization or approximate values. The horoscope at the same time provides the framework within which a person can and should develop.

In order to control the therapy process, a number of psychological tests can of course be given. I personally use the Luescher Color test, but the Rorschach test, the Szondi test, the Tu-Anima test and others may also be used. One should, however, never forget Dr. Heyer's classic remark, "He who cannot perceive, must test." Our principal diagnosis will begin later.

2. The Hypnosis

As early as the second session we take the next step: we start with hypnosis or relaxation training. After a short explanatory talk about the patient's attitude toward hypnosis, I employ the pendulum test. Here the patient holds a pendulum motionless in his hand. Underneath it, he sees a pane of glass inscribed with a circle surrounding a cross. I now ask him to concentrate on a specific direction (circular, vertical, or horizontal) and to imagine that the pendulum will swing in the desired direction. Within a short time, the pendulum will actually begin to move in the prescribed direction.

This phenomenon is a surprise to most patients and while we continue the experiment with variations, I can explain a number of things about the power of the performance. If the experiment succeeds (and it usually does) nothing further stands in the way of hypnosis. Should it not be a success on some occasion, this is a sign of resistance on the part of the patient either toward me or toward the treatment. In such cases, I attach to the patient the electrode of a small, highly sensitive galvanometer. While I ask a few pointed questions, the apparatus, by means of the psychogalvanic skin reflex (PSR), quickly indicates the location of unknown barriers that might obstruct the treatment. These are then made conscious and discharged. After this, the pendulum test, which failed previously, will certainly work. The patient then reclines on a comfortable couch and I start to induce hypnosis.

During the first session, I avoid all experiments except with body sensations such as rest, warmth, or weight. The patient must learn to relax and must not immediately be forced into a performance. Most persons expect too much from their first hypnosis session. Only when the patient realizes that nothing is actually happening, does he relax completely. Electronic meditation music makes it easier for many people to sink more deeply into hypnotic sleep.

As early as the first session, we frequently learn how well the patient takes to hypnosis. While one may have fallen into a deep hypnotic sleep, the other regrets that he was "still completely awake and heard everything."

It is important to make clear that hypnosis has nothing to do with unconsciousness but, on the contrary, requires an intensified consciousness. I usually compare hypnosis with the light beam from a flashlight. If the light passes through a concave lens, I will see relatively much, but it will be relatively unclear. If the light passes through a convex lens, I will see only a small dot, but it will be sharp and clear. The same thing happens in hypnosis. If consciousness corresponds to the concave light, hypnosis will greatly narrow this consciousnness in order to permit a specific point to become overly clear.

For further therapy, the depth of the patient's hypnosis is virtually unimportant. In deep hypnosis, regression is quick and easy to carry out. However, it is necessary for the patient to relax in a manner that will still enable him to clearly perceive weight and warmth. This can be achieved in a few sessions in every case.

In subsequent sessions I begin to suggest color experiences. The suggestion might be, "All by itself and without your help, a color will develop within your inner eye—it will be your color!" From the very beginning I am careful not to suggest any particular color in order to avoid the slightest activity or strain on the part of the patient. If I speak only of "your color," he is practically forced to wait and see what develops. Only when he is able to identify the first color clearly, do I go through the color chart: blue—green—yellow—orange—red—violet—blue. If the patient has difficulty seeing colors, I ask him to picture a meadow. Thus begins

3. *The Symbol Drama*

Depending on the ability of the patient, I run through, as quickly as possible, meadow, stream, spring, and delta. This technique and succession of pictures were clearly described by Professor Leuner in the concept of catathymic picture life. In addition to Professor Leuner's picture sequence, I especially like to make frequent use of the descent to the sea with magic wand and magic ring as described by Thomas. All in all, I use the symbol drama generously without depending on specific pictures. With the symbol drama, I attain three objectives simultaneously:

a. The patient learns the technique of daydreaming, that is, seeing pictures with his eyes closed, experiencing them, and talking about them at the same time. Since these inner pictures are projected "by themselves" without conscious assistance, the patient becomes accustomed to accepting material rising to the surface as it appears and to reporting it without criticism or comment. During these sessions the hypnotic state will deepen of its own accord.

b. The nature of the pictures permits a very good diagnosis of the actual state of the patient's psychic condition. The principle is similar to a projective test. Archetypal symbols are fed to the patient in the form of pictures that will then be shaped in accordance with his psychic structure. Since the symbolism is usually not known to the patient, a very accurate diagnosis of this picture world is thus made possible.

c. The symbol drama method, which in itself represents a therapeutic technique, begins to decrease the charge on the symbol level. This is already the beginning of therapy and is generally not recognized as such by the patient at this time, since the method is almost like playing games.

4. *The Birth*

Once the patient no longer has any difficulties with the picture life, I take him through his own birth. I take him, through the power of suggestion, back to the time of his birth and let him experience and describe the entire birth process. At this point, we almost always find physical feelings making their appearance. The patient experiences shortness of breath, pressure on his head, bodily pain, and the like. He smells the hospital odors, sees the delivery room, sees the people present, and hears every word that is spoken. For this, deep hypnosis is not necessary. The patient glides almost imperceptibly into this situation even when he himself believes it impossible. I have had the experience repeatedly that the patient, when I suggest to him, "Relive your birth," will start to explain why he cannot do it and suddenly break off in the middle of his excuse because he is already experiencing birth pains. The birth experience is repeated frequently because it becomes clearer with every repetition and more and more details are recognized each time.

Once the birth has become known, the therapy usually enters a new stage, since the patient has now learned of his own accord that there is nothing that is really forgotten and nothing that one cannot remember. He learns that there is no "cannot remember" but rather a "do not want to remember." He has now gained confidence and passively allows items to surface of their own accord without wanting to activate everything himself. It sometimes requires a great effort to convince a patient that everything will happen of its own accord if only he is prepared to let it do so. Many are of the opinion that they must enrich the therapy by clever analysis of their symptom, their childhood, their upbringing, and the like.

Our method, however, requires that all attempts at rational analysis be thwarted. This is also the reason why I do not attempt to jog the patient's memory at the start. Everything the patient knows and can describe is most certainly never the cause of his symptom. The sum total of everything a patient can tell me is that I then know what is definitely not the cause. Time, however, is too precious for this small reward. By virtue of a quick trip to the birth experience, I save a great deal of time since I pay practically no attention to events in this life following that time. We can retrieve this once we are certain that the patient is passively permitting his experiences to surface and to make his suppressed experiences known rather than, for the one hundredth time, warming up his favorite problems, which certainly possess no charge of any kind.

After the birth, we study the individual months of the embryonic stage in order to determine whether any trauma developed here. If we then conclude by examining the moment of conception, we shall have made known the greatest unknown portion of the current life. I make known to every patient his birth, his intrauterine condition, and his conception, regardless of his symptoms. Once the patient has reached this stage (this requires an average of ten sessions), nothing will stand in the way of the final technical step.

5. Incarnation Regression

As described previously, there are two methods of returning to the distant past of a patient. As in the case of his birth, pictures and events surface of their own accord, sometimes in a disorderly and chaotic fashion at first, but sometimes as an orderly and well-organized whole right from the start. Exerience will now help determine whether or not the patient finds himself on the level of the psychodrama. I have already described the criteria. The sessions are repeated and continued until the looked-for trauma (there can be more than one) appears and is experienced. Patient and therapist will each usually learn of his own accord whether the original trauma has been located within a certain specific experience, or whether the event was simply a temporary connecting link in the complex chain.

These sessions can be controlled with the previously mentioned instruments for measuring psychogalvanic skin reflexes, which can be of great help. With some experience, one can see from this instrument where a trauma is located, how great a charge it contains, whether it is ready to be confronted, and how much energy can be discharged. All these aids are not absolutely necessary, but when aimed at specific goals, they can frequently save the therapist and the patient a great deal of time. Using these time-saving methods, reincarnation therapy may sometimes require only thirty to sixty hours. Resistance, which may appear occasionally, is either a sign of a too highly charged event that one has approached, or may be the result of another problem temporarily overlapping the procedure. Resistance is handled in the same manner as the symptom itself. Energy charges that are too strong may be diminished to a safe level by inserting symbol dramas.

Throughout the therapy, entire sessions are sometimes devoted to dialogues that clarify questions that may arise. This will give the patient an insight into the basic laws of life and the universe. If these dialogues are carried on whenever they arise on their own from a particular therapy situation, it is easy for the patient to understand the connection, since he will have experienced the practical application within the session even before discussing the theory.

Psychotherapy is care of the soul. The technique of psychotherapy must be as thorough and as finely tuned as possible without being recognized as a technique by the patient. Human encounter, which enables the patient to learn to know himself, is the focal point of therapy. To the same extent, however, that a person gets to know himself, he gets to know his projection on the world around him, which up to now he always considered a reality coming from without. With every projection that he takes back with him, he accepts a bit more responsibility, but learns at the same time that the outside world is changing with him. One of the most important goals of my therapy is to have the patient learn, with time, that the environment by which he believes himself to be influenced is in reality only a reflection of himself. In this way, he obtains an effective instrument for changing the world—the way he wants to—simply by changing himself.

On this point I differ sharply with all sociological and sociopolitical philosophies that try to convince a person that he is the product of his environment. What a perversion of concepts! Man can never be the product of his environment; it is rather that society is a product of man. My patients do not believe this at the beginning, but fortunately they do not have to believe it, because they will experience it during therapy. At first, it is difficult for many to learn that no one in the world is to blame for their fate except themselves. In the end, however, this very understanding leads to a redeeming freedom.

All this proves that ideological and philosophical questions can by no means be banned from my therapy. Psychotherapy embraces the entire human being, touches the deepest levels of his existence. Psychotherapy must help a person find himself, understand himself, and make himself a significant part of the universe. Spiritual advisors are not therapists. Originally, ministry of the soul and medical science went hand in hand, both administered by a priest. By priest, I do not mean what we understand that title to mean today, but those wise men who understood the laws of nature and the cosmos and used this knowledge to help and to heal. The division of this occupation into churchmen, psychotherapists, and physicians was not in the best interests of mankind. A new combination of these three branches of knowledge would be a boon for suffering humanity. Psychotherapy today has the opportunity to further this development.

These final thoughts will hopefully avert the impression that reincarnation therapy is only a new therapeutic technique—rather, it is actually a new concept—which may possibly make its acceptance in professional circles more difficult.

The Claudia Case

H: We shall go backward through your life because time means nothing to us. Time is only a means of communication, a measure—but you will relive the past as if it were happening now. The past will become the present. We shall go backward in your life. You are getting younger; you will be twenty-five years old—we shall go back further; you will be twenty years old. Let us go back further—you are fifteen, ten years old. Today is your tenth birthday. How do you feel?

S: Not particularly well.

H: Why not?

S: I have the flu.

H: Did you get any presents?

S: Not many.

H: What did you get?

S: My mother sent me a package—a red blouse and a pleated gray skirt with straps—it has red and blue dots in it—but they took it from me.

H: Who took it from you?

S: My sister. She said the skirt was too short; it didn't fit me, so she gave it to some other girl. That was my birthday present [*cries*]—she, she doesn't like me—everything I get she gives away —she takes away everything, I can't keep anything [*cries*]— I don't like her either—I hate her—oh—I hate her [*cries*], I hate her, I hate her. [*cries*]

H: Let us dissolve from this birthday and go further back in time—we shall go further back in time. You are getting younger. You are now six years old. Are you going to school now?

S: Yes.

H: Can you do arithmetic?

S: Yes.

H: How much is five and five?

S: I have two hands—ten.

H: Good. Let us go back further. You are getting younger— five, four, three, two, one. Let us return to the moment of your birth. Today is April 13, 1946. You are just being born. What time is it?

S: Four fifty-two.

H: Good.

S: It is a Saturday, it's Saturday.

H: You are just being born. What do you feel? What is happening?

S: Phew, something is forcing me out.

H: Out of where?

S: Out of what I was in.

H: How does it look?

S: I don't know—dark and warm—but how does it look? You don't see it; you only feel it . . .

H: What do you feel?

S: Quite tight, but warm and soft.

H: Good. What happens next? You are just being born—tell me all your impressions exactly.

S: No, it won't work—I can't get out—I can't get out, I can hardly breathe—I—no, it's not that I can't breathe, but—I don't know—I can't get out—I must get out—but it won't work, but suddenly it's getting light and something is lifting me up—a woman is lying on the table—it's my mother, and another doctor is taking something out—and her stomach is open—and there I am, I got out.

H: From where did you get out?

S: Out of the stomach—the open stomach, it's bleeding and now I'm getting a—hmm [*laughs*] and the midwife, or whoever it is—yes, midwife—keeps saying, "My God, what a beautiful child—with such beautiful blue eyes"—I don't even know whether I have blue eyes—hm.

H: Did something go wrong with your birth?

S: No, no, I don't think so, I can't imagine what.

H: Were you born by Caesarean section?

S: I don't know what they call it, but in my case, they cut open the woman's stomach and I came out.

H: Let us go back further in time. Let us return to the cave from which you came—to the time of conception—Why are you laughing? Tell me!

S: Hm [*laughs*] nothing—but it keeps bouncing.

H: Tell me exactly—what is bouncing?

S: I don't know, hm, hm.

H: What is happening?

S: Yes, I am lying there and it keeps bouncing—I think, I have—no—that can't be—no, that can't be, I have experienced it before, this bouncing, but I'm not even born yet.

H: Tell me what is happening. Describe all your experiences.

S: It is pleasant, it is wonderfully pleasant, warm and soft, and even when it bounces, it is soft, it doesn't hurt—and I keep thinking—but perhaps it's only my imagination—I have experienced this bouncing around once before, or I know what it is.

H: What is it?

S: Like being on a wagon, or on a wagon rolling over stones.

H: Good, dissolve back to that picture.

S: Yes, I [*coughs*] . . .

H: What's the matter; why are you coughing?

S: I'm sick; I was in a wagon with the gentleman—in a horse and wagon—I have to cough constantly.

H: What is your name?

S: Claudia—that comes from Claudine—because Mama says—that way it won't be noticed—

H: What won't be noticed?

S: At the time when I was born—there were many Frenchmen in the area—they were Napoleon's troops—and Mama, Mama called me Claudine—so that everyone would think—a Frenchman was my father—

H: Why were they supposed to think that?

S: No one was to know that the gentleman was my father.

H: What gentleman?

S: Well, the gentleman, the baron.

H: What sort of baron is he?

S: Hm, Baron von Redwitz, but he's already married.

H: Why do you call him "the gentleman"?

S: Because my mother works for him.

H: What sort of work does she do?

S: She sews for Charlotte and for his wife.

H: Who is Charlotte?

S: Charlotte is the daughter.

H: Whose daughter?

S: The daughter of the gentleman and his wife.

H: And this gentleman is your father?

S: Yes, but I'm not allowed to tell anyone. You must not tell anyone, either.

H: How do you know that?

S: Mama told me, but I didn't always know it. I only knew it since I was thirteen.

H: And how old are you now?

S: I am thirteen, and we are riding in the coach, the horse-drawn coach.

H: Where to?

S: To Berlin.

H: When were you born?

S: September 12, 1810, no 1812; Charlotte was born in 1810 [*moans*].

H: Do you like Charlotte?

S: Yes, she is a dear—she always helps me if there is something I can't do.

H: Do you go to school?

S: Yes, but not to school—we have a tutor.

H: Who are we?

S: Charlotte and I.

H: What are you learning?

S: Everything possible, arithmetic, writing, French—but I don't like to learn French—I always say, "madmosell"—then she pushes me into bed and says, "You'd better rest"—because she knows I'm sick.

H: What's wrong with you?

S: The doctor says consumption.

H: What is that, anyway? How does that feel?

S: Hm, it's hard to breathe, you always have to cough, and it hurts when you cough, and I'm terribly thin.

H: You are now riding in the coach. Where are you riding to?

S: To Berlin.

H: What do you intend to do in Berlin?

S: I want to see the King.

H: Where are you coming from?

S: From Ratibor.

H: What's that name?

S: Ratibor.

H: Where is that?

S: In Silesia.

H: Is it a big town?

S: No, not too big.

H: And you are on your way to Berlin?

S: Yes.

H: And what are you going to do in Berlin?

S: I want to see the King!

H: Which King?

S: Well, Frederick Wilhelm!

H: Why do you want to see him?

S: Because I made a wish, because I want to see how he looks —and Papa—the gentleman—said, the next time he goes to Berlin, he will take me along—and so—now we are on our way to Berlin.

H: Do you call him Papa or sir?

S: I call him Papa only when we are alone.

H: And at other times?

S: Then I call him Mr. Redwitz.

H: And you are now on your way to Berlin.

S: Yes.

H: What are you riding in? Is that a big automobile?

S: What did you say?

H: Is that a big auto or is it a bus?

S: A what? It's a—I told you we are riding in a horse-drawn coach.

H: In a horse-drawn coach?

S: Yes.

H: How many horses are there?

S: Four.

H: Good, so we shall arrive in Berlin.

S: Yes.

H: Tell me what happens now.

S: I—there is some sort of procession—and it's cold—it's winter —I'm freezing and the gentleman is taking me in his arms and wrapping me in his coat—hm—there comes the coach with the King—I—hm—I didn't need to see him—he's real old and ugly—I always thought a King was young and handsome, but this one —he's old—and I'm disappointed.

H: Is the Queen there, too?

S: No, she died—she's been dead a long time. Papa said—the gentleman said—she died before I was born—when Charlotte was born.

H: You don't like the King?

S: No.

H: How does he look?

S: Oh, he's—bah—he's old—he's so—I don't know, such a peculiar chin, no, he doesn't even have a chin—he has a—it just goes right from the mouth to the neck, then he has a great big nose— [*laughs*]—but Papa says one must not laugh at a king—yes, he said princes and kings are not always young and handsome—but I still had to laugh at the way he looked—he certainly isn't handsome—but I like it on his birthday—

H: What do you like?

S: We always get something.

H: What do you get?

S: Oh, presents.

H: From whom?

S: He has them distributed—it's sort of a celebration—always in summer.

H: When is his birthday?

S: In August.

H: And what sort of presents do you get?

S: All kinds of knickknacks.

H: For example?

S: On the square they build stands—and they distribute slips of paper—you know—slips with something written on them, a number or a name, or something like that and you go to the stands, and they look at the slips to see what it says on them, and then you get something—I once got a necklace.

H: Do you know the exact date of the King's birthday?

S: Yes, I believe it's August 8.

H: Good. Now you have seen the King.

S: Hm—yes.

H: What else are you doing in Berlin?

S: Not much more—the gentleman—the gentleman is buying something—something for the animals—but I don't know what it is—

H: What could it be?

S: Well—so that they stay healthy or get healthy or strong or something like that.

H: What sort of animals?

S: Well, the horses and cows—from the farm, you know. We have quite a few animals.

H: Which ones do you like the most?

S: Oh, horses.

H: Can you ride?

S: Well, yes, but not too well, because I can't hold on.

H: Why can't you?

S: Didn't I tell you that?

H: No.

S: Well, my left arm is lame.

H: Can't you move it?

S: No—I always have to—I don't know—Mama always said— she used to, not anymore—that is the punishment.

H: For what?

S: Well, what she did.

H: What did she do?

S: Well, because what she did with the gentleman—but we don't talk about that.

H: What is the connection with the arm?

S: What connection?

H: The connection between what your mother did and your crippled or lame arm?

S: Well, Mama said that is the punishment for her sin, because she was not married to the gentleman—he already had a wife then, and also a child—Charlotte.

H: And you cannot move the arm at all?

S: No, I always have to lift it up with the other hand like this and close the fingers, then I can hold something with it, but I don't feel anything. You know, the doctor always pricks it with a pin, but I don't feel anything—he always says it won't get any better.

H: Can you write?

S: Yes, I can write, because I write with the other hand.

H: With which hand do you write?

S: Well, with the right hand, since the left hand won't work.

H: Can you write something for me?

S: Yes, what?

H: Your name.

S: Yes.

H: Here is something to write on.

H: Very good. What does it say?

S: Well, Roeder, I told you.

H: Roeder?

S: Yes.

H: Your name is Claudia Roeder?

S: Yes.

H: Let us go back further in time. You are getting younger, you are ten, eight, six, four, two years old, you are just being born. What is the date?

S: September 12, 1812.

H: You are just being born. What time is it?

S: I don't know that; we have no clock.

H: But you still know what time it is.

S: No, we don't have a clock. How can I tell, we have no clock.

H: The correct time—to the minute—it will come to you— what time is it? It is the moment of your birth!

S: Oh, I—it is so far away—yes, one minute to four.

H: In the morning or afternoon?

S: It is dark, it is dark; yes, I am being born now.

H: What's the matter? Tell me!

S: Well, she, she's holding me so strangely—

H: Who is holding you strangely?

S: This old lady, this woman, and she keeps saying, "Poor little creature, such a poor little creature." Well, I guess I look pretty scrawny.

H: What other voices do you hear?

S: None, only this old lady, she talks funny, "Such a poor little creature."

H: Whom does she mean by that?

S: Well, me!

H: Why are you poor?

S: No, I'm not poor, just a little scrawny, you know, well, maybe a little small.

H: But otherwise you are well?

S: Yes, I think so; I cry quite well.

H: Do you like it here on earth?

S: No, not at all.

H: Why not?

S: It is cold, and the woman who always talks so strangely, I wish she would say something else; that's terrible and, no—I don't know, I just don't like it.

H: Do you like your mother?

S: Oh, yes, Mama is beautiful, very beautiful—but not at the moment.

H: Why not?

S: I think it took a lot out of her; she looks tired and pale.

H: Let us go back, back to the time before your birth; how do you like it here?

S: Fine.

H: How is it here?

S: Well, here I can do what I want—

H: What are you doing?

S: Oh, just kicking around.

H: Why do you do that?

S: I don't know, it's fun, and wherever you kick, it's soft—and it gives—and you can't get hurt, and it's warm, you know, comfy and cozy.

H: Is that how it is?

S: I think so, yes.

H: Good. Let's go back a bit further; go back until your present condition changes—let's keep going back until you come across a new situation—what do you see?

S: [*moans*] My God—no, oh no, oh no.

H: What's the matter?

S: It disgusts me.

H: What is it?

S: Ha, the rats, oh, no—help!

H: First tell me where you are!

S: Oh, my God [*cries*]—I'm in a tower [*cries*]—I, no—the—

H: Tell me, what do you see here?

S: Rats, rats, phew—oh, no—

H: Why are you here in this tower? What sort of tower is this? How did you get in here?

S: They threw me in [*moans*].

H: Let us go back a bit further in time—let us go back to before you were in the tower. Tell me something of your life. Where are you; what are you doing?

S: I am, we are out of the house—not house, but hut—we had to leave.

H: Why?

S: Because they were looking for my husband.

H: Why are they looking for him?

S: Well, he wants to fight against the duke—he wants to kill him.

H: Your husband wants to kill the duke?

S: Yes.

H: Why?

S: Well, because he takes everything away from the people —you can just barely stay alive—everything else he takes away.

H: What is the duke's name?

S: I don't know.

H: Where do you live with your husband?

S: In the Koehler Valley.

H: Where is that?

S: There—in, well, in the Black Forest—the people only call it the "black forest."

H: Do you know of any city nearby?

S: Yes, there is a town where they have—well—healing water —you know, they say when you drink it, you stay healthy.

H: What is your name?

S: Mine?

H: Yes.

S: My name is Lena.

H: What else?

S: Nothing else, but the people call me "black Lena."

H: Why do they call you black?

S: Because I have long black hair.

H: How old are you?

S: I am twenty-six.

H: What year it this?

S: 1720—

H: What year is it?

S: 1723, I think.

H: When were you born?

S: Before the turn of the century.

H: How many years before?

S: I don't know exactly, I think maybe three years.

H: Were you born in 1697?

S: That may be.

H: You are now twenty-six years old?

S: Yes, and now is—I have to think—I'm not very smart.

H: Can you write?

S: No, I can't write.

H: Just a little bit?

S: No, I only know numbers that I have seen somewhere, but I don't know, I think they're numbers, but I don't know what that means.

H: Can you write them for me the way you saw them?

S: Yes.

H: Here is something for you to write on.

S: You want me to copy this?

H: Yes, copy it!

S: I can't just do it like that—first I have to look—and see what it looks like.

H: Yes, look at it and copy it.

S: Well—it's difficult—now there's something, I don't think I can do that—well, I'll try, it's like this ◯ and like this ୫ .

H: Two circles, one above the other?

S: Yes, a little one on top and a big one on the bottom, a little circle on top, do you see?

H: Yes.

S: Yes, but I don't know what it is—I think it's a number, and then there is—you know, I always wanted to learn that, but there's no one here to teach you. How does it go? Like this and like this and like this. It's written on the wall, you know; I'm reading it from this wall.

H: What sort of wall is that?

S: It belongs to the castle.

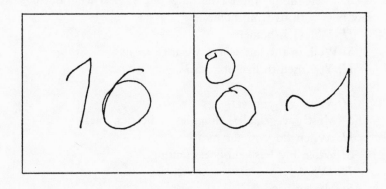

H: It says 1687.

S: I don't know what it says; I only copied it—but I can't write my name.

H: You did that very well, thank you. Do you always speak the way you are speaking to me now?

S: Yes.

H: Do you talk like that to other people too?

S: Yes, we have our own language.

H: Then talk to me in that language.

S: All right.

H: Tell me something—where do you live?

S: [*Starts to speak in a very broad Swabian dialect*] I've already told you.

H: Where is it?

S: In the Koehler Valley.

H: Yes, do you have a house? Where do you live there?

S: We used to live in a hut—but since they're after my husband we've been hiding. You know, it's not a house—it's made of stones—it looks like a house, but it isn't—but when it rains—well, you're a little—at least we're dry.

H: How does it look inside?

S: Well, inside there's nothing but stones—we just took a few rags with us from home.

H: Where is home?

S: Well, in the hut where we used to live.

H: You used to live in a hut?

S: Yes.

H: What do you eat?

S: Mostly vegetables, dumplings, berries, meat.

H: When do you eat meat?

S: When my husband goes hunting!

H: Who?

S: My husband.

H: What does he hunt?

S: Mostly rabbits.

H: Does he shoot them?

S: Well, he has some sort of—sort of an apparatus, I don't know what it's called.

H: What does it look like?

S: Well, first it was a bow and arrow, and then they made it simpler. Well, it looks like a bow and arrow, but it isn't a bow and arrow, it's something else, but I don't know what it's called.

H: Very well, tell me something about your husband.

S: Yes, he's a fool—he [*laughs*]—but don't tell him—I like him anyway—he is—he thinks if he kills the duke, things will get better, but I doubt it—and he will have to suffer—I told him that—and the next one will do exactly the same thing.

H: Are there others or is your husband doing this all alone?

S: Oh, yes, there are lots of others with him, but—

H: What do the people call your husband?

S: Well, his name is Hans.

H: And what do they call him?

S: Nothing, his name is Hans and that's what they call him.

H: What was his trade before he became a rebel?

S: A charcoal burner. What was that? What did you call him?

H: Isn't he a rebel?

S: What is that? No, you know, he—what is this—a rebel? No, I think they call him something else.

H: What is it? What do they call him?

S: Well, a revolutionary, I guess.

H: And what did he used to do?

S: He used to have a charcoal kiln.

H: What did he have?

S: A charcoal kiln.

H: Did you know him then?

S: Of course, we have two children.

H: What are your children's names?

S: Gregory and Tami.

H: Gregory and Tami?

S: Yes, Gregory is the older one.

H: Are they both boys?

S: Yes.

H: How old is Gregory?

S: Gregory is ten and Tami is about eight; well, he was born just about two years after Gregory.

H: After whom?

S: After Gregory.

H: Tell me, you're now fleeing, or are you in hiding at the moment?

S: I guess we're in hiding.

H: You have the children with you?

S: Yes, I have the children, but Hansi isn't here.

H: Where is he?

S: He is somewhere else—I sent him on.

H: Why?

S: So that they won't find him.

H: And how are you doing?

S: Oh, my feet, my feet hurt.

H: Why?

S: Because I've walked so far, but you know, I'm tired of—how do you say that—the way we did it was—you know, I'm so close to the castle with Gregory and Tami that the duke will never suspect; he's looking for us much further away—he thinks we ran away, but instead we're right near the castle—and he doesn't know it—we sure fooled him—ha, ha—every day they run right past us—but I have to make sure the children keep their mouths shut.

H: Who runs past?

S: The people who are looking for my husband.

H: And who are they?

S: The duke's guards or something like that—how do they—what did you say? How do they look? You mean what do they look like, right?

H: Yes.

S: Well, how do they look, hm, tight pants and a jacket, tight pants and knee-length boots.

H: What color is the jacket?

S: Red, yes, the jackets are red.

H: Very well, now tell me what else is happening to you. They are looking for you and then what happens? Let us move forward in time.

S: Well I'm—my husband hasn't come back, he's, he's hiding

—I told him to go to my friend—the one who lives near the place where the water is.

H: Do you know the name of the place?

S: Well, sort of, but one says Bad Teilach or Teinach and the other just calls it Teinach.

H: And that's where your husband is now?

S: Somewhere near there, yes.

H: What happens to you now?

S: Well, we have nothing more to eat—and—I'm going into the woods to see if maybe I can catch a rabbit or something.

H: How do you do that?

S: Ha, with a cord.

H: How does that work?

S: You just have to wait, you know—you make a snare—and I know where the rabbits usually run—where they, how do you say that—where their—well, where they always go, and there you lay the trap and wait and wait and wait—and the snare simply hangs there—you just have to keep trying—so I hang it there and wait until a rabbit runs through it—but most of the time it doesn't work—because—ha—the rabbits are pretty fast, you know, and they're not so dumb—but once I caught one— my, did he struggle—now I'm going into the woods and see if I can find something to eat—the children are hungry—they have—

H: Did you ever in your life have money?

S: Money? No—that, that's for paying—I know it, but we don't have any. You know, we don't have anything like that.

H: What happens next to you and your children?

S: Well, I'm in the woods now, trying to find something to eat.

H: Any luck?

S: No, no—they're coming . . .

H: Who's coming?

S: The duke's guards.

H: And?

S: Now I'm going to run like—I'm pretty fast, I can run

fast—but they have—their wind is better—at first it looks pretty good, but I can't—how do you say that?—run anymore—they're getting closer all the time—now they've got me—there's nothing else I can do—

H: What are they doing, now that they have you?

S: Hm, hm [*moans*] . . .

H: Tell me what's happening—come, tell me—look at the whole picture.

S: They're not going to get me—they won't get me, but they did get me—I'm fighting like the devil—but there's four of them—four, I think—I can't count, but there's as many as my whole hand, if you take away the thumb—that's how many there are—and they're much stronger than I am . . .

H: What are they doing with you?

S: They're holding on to me and taking me to that character—to the duke.

H: Yes, and what happens now?

S: Well, the Englishman is there again.

H: Which Englishman?

S: The duke has a visitor or something—

H: How do you know that?

S: He's a real foreigner—he was always after me—the swine—he informed on me.

H: Tell me something about him.

S: He was the only one who knew where I was, yes, we met in the forest—and he talked so funny—I couldn't understand him—right, right or oke, that's all he ever said—he always kept saying oke—always . . .

H: And what did you say?

S: Well, I tried to talk to him normally, like I'm talking to you—but he couldn't understand me—he—he—I tried to be sensible—actually—and he kept coming after me—he knew my husband was away—and he wanted to—he—he—hm—he wanted to do something to me—you know what I mean . . .

H: What did he want?

134—

S: Well, hm—

H: Well, what did he want?

S: I can't tell you that; you know what I mean.

H: And he is there, too, where they took you prisoner now?

S: He is in the castle with the duke, talking to him in his strange language—

H: And what happens to you now?

S: Well, they're beating me now—and how—and they want to know where my husband is—but—[*moans*]—but I won't tell them—[*moans*]—and now they're throwing me into the tower where the rats are—I get nothing to eat—and the weaker I get, the nearer they come to me—I can't scare them away—now— eh—[*moans*].

H: Tell me, what is it?

S: I want them to go away.

H: I beg your pardon?

S: I want them to go away—the rats—they're eating at me— they're eating at my feet—bah—disgusting—

H: Describe what you see.

S: Oh, that—[*moans*]

H: Look closely!

S: You want me to look at that? [*moans*]

H: Look at it!

S: I can't look at it.

H: Tell me what colors you see.

S: They're black—black—oh—

H: More.

S: Oh [*expresses disgust*].

H: Don't smell, look!

S: Oh, me.

H: Tell we what is happening.

S: They're eating me—

H: Look closely.

S: Bah—

H: Look closely.

S: But that I—you're asking a lot—you want me to watch them eat me, but how . . .

H: Don't be disgusted—just look—have you looked?

S: Yes.

H: Very well, then continue—what else is happening? Tell me, what else is happening to you?

S: I am becoming unconscious.

H: How does that feel?

S: Fine—now I don't feel anything.

H: Can you still see it?

S: Yes, I see it—but I'm not there—that is—I am there, but—I see myself.

H: What is that—what does that mean?

S: Ah—I'm dead— hah [*breathes a sigh of relief*].

H: Come, tell me, what's happening?

S: They let me starve to death—now they're coming down the steps—one is kicking me—no, not me, but my body, that's lying there—he's kicking me in the side with his foot and says he wants me to get up and come along, but of course I can't do that—I'm dead—then one of them says, "I guess she's gone," or something like that, and the big rat is still eating at my body.

H: Now, when you watch the rats eating you, what do you feel?

S: Nothing—that's just the shell—they're eating my shell—that doesn't bother me. If they're always down there, they must get hungry—they don't get anything to eat, so let them eat—I don't feel anything anymore.

H: What are you doing now?

S: Well, I'm going to look for my husband—he's still in my friend's hut—and he has a girl or a woman, I can't tell exactly—he has her in his arms—they're laughing and they seem to be having a good time—no more talk of killing the duke or insurrection—they're just having a good time and drinking and laughing.

H: How does that affect you?

S: It doesn't bother me at all—if he enjoys it—if he's satisfied and happy—let him be.

H: What will you do now?

S: Well, I'm going to—I must see what my children are doing —the little one is crying—I'm stroking his hair and trying to take him in my arms—but I don't think he notices it—and the big one, Gregory, keeps talking to him—

H: What is he saying?

S: He is saying, "Watch and see, Mama will be back soon," and Tami says, "But she's been gone so long and I'm hungry."

H: How does this make you feel?

S: I don't know, I don't know what it means to feel—they're my children, but I, I feel nothing toward them.

H: Very well, what happens now?

S: Well, I can see and recognize everything, but I am everywhere and nowhere—you know—this is a state—how can I explain it—everything is smooth and quiet—and you can wish to be wherever you want—and suddenly you're there—simply by thinking—after all, you no longer have a body.

H: Would you like to remain in this state?

S: I don't know.

H: What happens next?

S: I think—I think I will get a new body.

H: When will that be?

S: Well, for a human it might be a long time, but for us it's not long.

H: Who are you?

S: Well, we're—what are we—we, yes, I don't know what we are—we have thoughts—we are, we are thoughts—I believe we are just thoughts—without a body, but I can't tell you exactly.

H: Is it pleasant—this state?

S: Yes, but, pleasant, pleasant—you know, what is called life and what happens during this life—this is—how shall I say it— at present it's harmonious and smooth and quiet, but there are no highs and lows—you know, you might say it's monotonous—

I think—you are human, and humans in this state—that—I don't know, I'm quite certain you would find it very monotonous.

H: Do you find it monotonous?

S: Well, I, hm, I don't know what to tell you, it's pleasant and—but I, I think I will want to leave here at some time—you know, there are others here who don't want to leave anymore, and they don't have to leave, they can stay—because they're—they've grown accustomed to this place—you know—they know it will always be like this—and they're satisfied and content—yes, really content, they don't want it any other way—but I—I don't know—I think after a few hundred years I might find it monotonous—I think—I will want to leave sometime—I'm not yet ready—I haven't reached the point where, as some of them here say, "We shall stay"—can you understand that? Do you really understand that? You're a human being.

H: I shall try to understand you.

S: Yes, but you know, I can't explain it so well, I—if I had a body now, I could probably explain it to you better—you know—but I am nothing now—I am only—what am I, anyway? Do you know what I am?

H: What are you?

S: Do you know what I am? Can you tell me what I am now?

H: Are you not simply yourself?

S: Yes, I am myself—but what am I made of? Out of, hm, I don't know—out of air? or, hm . . .

H: What could we call what you are made of?

S: Energy maybe, I don't know whether you understand. It may be energy—but I don't know exactly—I . . .

H: Good, then you want to come back into the world once more?

S: Yes, I guess so, but I don't want another body that has to, that has to suffer so much—

H: Do you have a choice?

S: No, I don't.

H: What will the new life be like?

S: Short, very short.

H: Why short?

S: Well, I'll have to suffer again—just what I didn't want—the body will have to suffer again, but not the soul—only the body—but the soul will—I think—be pretty well smoothed out—or I, you know, what I am right now—when that's inside a body—the body may suffer—but that, which I am, won't suffer—it will remain at peace and . . .

H: Is that better?

S: Yes, much.

H: Good, then let's go forward to this change—let's proceed to that point in time when you are united with your body again—how does it feel?

S: Well, hm, the feeling—that is, there is no feeling—it is only—you can't call it a feeling—if you—if I have a body and you pinch me, I feel it, but what is happening now is not a feeling—hm, well—I don't know how to explain it.

H: Have you been reunited with matter?

S: No, not yet.

H: Where are you?

S: Well, I'm—well, where am I?—everywhere and nowhere.

H: All right, let's proceed to the point where you are reunited with matter.

S: That is—I'll have to—I'll have to enter there.

H: Enter where?

S: Into this union.

H: Is it difficult?

S: No, not difficult, but—it doesn't hurt, either, at least it's not unpleasant—but I don't know how to explain it—imagine—imagine this huge vacuum cleaner—and it sucks you in or something like that—something like that, yes, but it doesn't hurt—it isn't unpleasant either, it really isn't.

H: What's happening to you now?

S: Well, now I'm entering into it—I'm making the connection.

H: What else is happening?

S: I still have no body, but the thing I am in is growing—but very slowly—it's as if—you know, as if somebody is slowly pulling on all your limbs, very slowly and suddenly—I wouldn't say it's unpleasant—and suddenly you have a shape again.

H: Can you see your future life?

S: Yes.

H: Do you know about your arm?

S: Yes.

H: How did you get this arm that you can't move?

S: Well, this—I don't know—this woman in which I am—this woman who is to become my mother—she must have somehow either fallen or been kicked—I don't know—but I believe someone or something kicked her.

H: Dissolve back to that incident.

S: But I can't see that.

H: You will be able to see it; describe what is happening.

S: Well, Mama is in the stable with—with the gentleman who is my father—and she is talking to him—oh—and she is really quite composed—you know—hm—but the man starts to get excited and waves his arms around and starts shouting, and the horses are restless—and Mama gets real close to him and he, oh, he pushes her away.

H: Describe how he pushes her.

S: He—Mama—or rather the woman in whose body I am—who is to become my mother—she wants to go to him and embrace him—but I can't hear what they're saying—what they're talking about—he just pushes her away and puts her arms down—and she falls backward against the horse—the horse is frightened and kicks—and kicks the woman in the stomach.

H: What do you feel?

S: I feel, I feel—I don't know—it's as if I'm deaf—I feel numb—you know—as if I still don't exist and yet I do—I still don't have a body—not a real one—I'm still incomplete—and this incomplete being is—you know, just numb.

H: Is the kick the cause of your lame arm?

S: Yes—it just hit me in the shoulder.

H: Very well, let us go on—let us proceed to the moment of your birth—you are being born.

S: Yes, I must get out—out of where I am now—out of this woman's body—and then she will be my mother.

H: Does this woman look familiar? Can it be that you were together with this woman in some former life?

S: No, not with her.

H: But do any of the other people whom you see look familiar to you?

S: Yes, yes, there is a little child, a little girl—maybe two years old—I must have seen her somewhere before.

H: Dissolve into the past—who was she previously? Look at your previous life. Where else have you seen her?

S: She was my sister—but she is not the child of the mother who has now brought me into the world—no, that child belongs to a different woman—that child belongs to the wife of the gentleman—but, hm, no, that . . .

H: She was your sister in your prior life?

S: Yes.

H: Do you recognize this gentleman; can you find him somewhere in your past?

S: No, I have never seen him, but the little girl—yes, I know the little girl—she drowned—she drowned in the stream that flows past our house.

H: Then?

S: Yes, in the Koehler Valley.

H: How old was she at that time?

S: She was about four then—but I . . .

H: Was it your fault that she drowned?

S: No, no, that's impossible; it couldn't have been my fault.

H: Is she older than you?

S: Yes, I was only—I couldn't—I can't even walk yet . . .

H: Very well, let us return to this girl, to this life that you are just starting—so she is the daughter of the man who is also your father?

S: Yes, but actually at this time I don't know that he is my father.

H: You will only know this later?

S: Yes, I won't know it until I'm about thirteen years old.

H: You don't know it at present?

S: No, I don't.

H: Let us go forward in your life—let us go to your thirteenth year, when you find out about it. You are growing older, getting bigger—you are now thirteen years old—correct?

S: Correct.

H: How old will you get to be?

S: I will not get to be very old; I may have about another half-year to live, not much more.

H: Very well, let us go forward in time until just before your death.

S: Yes.

H: Tell me what happens.

S: Well, I am lying on the bed and I'm terribly thin and frail, I, hm, and the doctor is there and says he can't help me anymore—I'll have to die.

H: Very well, let's do that.

S: Yes.

H: What is happening?

S: Not much—it is, hm, like falling asleep, sort of like—it's not a battle—such as I experienced once before.

H: You mean in the tower.

S: Yes, now it's only, only falling asleep—you know, I will simply fall asleep and not wake up again, and Mama is over me, stroking my hair and crying, and Charlotte is there, too—she's crying, too—I think she liked me—

H: Tell me the date you died.

S: It is winter—January.

H: January what?

S: I can't say exactly; it's 1826.

H: What day in January?

S: The thirteenth or fifteenth.

H: Is it the thirteenth?

S: It could be the fifteenth; it's the thirteenth.

H: Is it January 13, 18 . . . ?

S: 1826.

H: At what time of day did you die?

S: It is noon, afternoon.

H: Is it three o'clock, two o'clock?

S: Later.

H: Later than three o'clock?

S: Yes, but we have no clock, I'll have to . . .

H: The time will appear as a number. Read it!

S: It is 4:28 P.M.

H: Thank you. What happens now?

S: I am going to Mama and stroke her hair—you know, she always used to say to me, "It won't be so bad when I die, I shall return and you will return," so now when I go to stroke her hair and she is crying so bitterly, I say to her, "Mama, you know I'll return"—but she can't hear me.

H: What else do you see? Your mother and what else?

S: Yes and my—she is lying on top of me—on top of my body, which is still in the bed, and she is brushing the hair out of my eyes and keeps saying, "Dear God, why?" and keeps asking "Dear God, why did it have to happen to me? I did no evil," or something like that, because she has already been punished for her sin.

H: How?

S: Well, you know, that's why I got the lame arm.

H: How are you doing now?

S: Oh, I'm fine—I'm back where I came from.

H: Was your past life worthwhile for you?

S: For me, yes—I'm—nothing really much happened—I couldn't do what I wanted to—I couldn't run and jump like other children—but I could swim and ride and play with all the animals that were there and yes, I believe it was worthwhile—I was never dissatisfied with my life—I simply took it as it came, and it was very nice.

H: What happens to you now? Will you remain in this state?

S: No, I doubt that.

H: Why?

S: Well, it was much too short. You know, what I experienced now—the—what do you call that?—hm, it purified me—but it was much too short, it was . . .

H: You will come back to earth?

S: I'm sure of it, yes.

H: What will you still have to learn?

S: Well, I'll have to learn to accept fate as it comes—you know, make the best of it—come what may—and not always say—you know, let me give you an example: I have—when I'm very thirsty, yes, and I see a glass half-full of water—I must not say it's half-empty—but I must say, "Thank God, it's still half-full"—you know, that's what I must learn—do you understand what I mean?

H: Will you learn that in your coming life?

S: I think so, and I'll have to learn to swallow or put up with a great deal—or whatever you want to call it—but I really believe I will learn that in this life.

H: So you really want to be born again?

S: I don't want to, but I have to.

H: Good, let's proceed to the point in time where you are united with matter again.

S: Yes.

H: Relive your conception.

S: There is the big vacuum cleaner again—you know, I've told you about that already—don't you remember?

H: Yes, I do.

S: Well—that's—you know—hm, but I don't want to go there at all.

H: Where?

S: Well, where I'm supposed to go.

H: You don't want to go?

S: No.

H: Why not?

S: I don't know—I don't think it will work—I don't know why—I can't explain it—but—

H: But you will get there?

S: I will get there, I must get there; it has been predetermined —yes, you know—well, it's simply been preordained.

H: Good, have you now been reunited with matter?

S: Yes, I have.

H: And you're beginning to grow?

S: Yes.

H: Let us proceed to the moment of your birth. You are just being born.

S: Hm, well, this is a tight situation—you know, I'm quite big and I must get out—and it can't be done—with this woman it just won't work.

H: What happens next?

S: It's getting light now, now they're lifting me out, yes, out of the stomach, it's been cut open—yes.

H: Look at your mother and look at the people with whom you will come in contact in your new life—do any of them look familiar? Have you met any of them in a previous life?

S: Not my mother, definitely not my mother.

H: Your former father? This Mr. von Redwitz? Will you meet him again?

S: It's possible, but I doubt if I would recognize him again.

H: Look over your life and see whether you won't meet him again. Will you meet him again?

S: No, we won't meet again, but he's there—in a, in a different city.

H: Tell me the name of the city.

S: Ah, it could be Cologne—there is a—yes, I believe it is Cologne—there is a cathedral—and there is—this man is in Cologne —hm, well—I don't know—he's there, but his name is not Redwitz—he has a different name—

H: Do you know what his name is now?

S: No, I don't, but I know what he looks like.

H: What is he doing in Cologne?

S: I don't know, maybe he's a doctor or something like that —perhaps he's a veterinarian or something.

H: But your paths won't cross?

S: No, definitely not. We won't see each other.

H: You are now born and are growing up.

S: Yes.

H: Let us go forward in time to the year 1975, all right?

S: Yes.

H: Let us stop on May 11, 1975.

S: Yes, today is Mother's Day.

H: Yes, today is May 11, 1975. You are sleeping soundly and peacefully; you are in a deep hypnotic sleep. We have spoken about many things and have taken a long trip, but everything we have discussed will attach itself to your conscious being and will be known to you even after this session—everything we have talked about, everything that you have experienced, everything you have seen, all this will be at your disposal after the session— is this agreeable to you?

S: Yes.

H: Look back over your previous development, review your past that we have discussed. How does it feel to see the past close up, to recognize it and to look over it?

S: Well, it's a—knowledge that everyone ought to have— everyone ought to know what he was or is.

H: So you will find it agreeable and pleasant?

S: Yes, only—there is something—

H: What else is there?

S: The rats.

H: Hm, what about them?

S: They—rats disgust me—when I see a rat, my flesh creeps.

H: Why?

S: You know—that rats were once eating me?

H: Yes, and you know it now, too.

S: Yes, and every time I see a rat . . .

H: You relive what you experienced a long time ago.

S: No, I don't know whether I relive it—but, in any case, it disgusts me terribly.

H: And this aversion started at that time?

S: Yes.

H: Now every time you see a rat, you must coordinate the time correctly; you know that this aversion goes back two hundred years; it has no business in your current life. You will learn to like rats—you will find them pleasant, beautiful.

S: Ah—

H: This feeling belongs back two centuries.

S: Do you really believe that?

H: Where does this feeling belong?

S: Do you really believe that? Learn to like rats?

H: Rats disgust you?

S: Yes.

H: Very well, where does this aversion belong? Dissolve back!

S: Yes, 1725.

H: Return to that situation!

S: No.

H: You must learn to look at it—not so much disgust, not so much emotion—don't show your feelings—look at it and describe it—look at it objectively—what is happening—the rats are nibbling at you, correct?

S: Yes, at my feet.

H: Yes, and why? Because they are hungry.

S: Yes, because they're hungry.

H: What's so bad about that?

S: But why are they eating me?

H: Why should we ask that?

S: Well, I still feel it.

H: Yes, but the rats are hungry.

S: Yes.

H: Learn how to turn it around. What is happening objectively?

S: Well, I feel the pain when they gnaw on me.

H: You are being eaten by rats, but earlier you ate a rabbit.

S: That's right.

H: What is happening objectively?

S: I was—I was hungry, too—and killed the rabbit—but the rats aren't actually killing me—I'm wrong—they, I'm almost dead—they let me starve—I have no water and no food—

H: Is that the rats' fault?

S: No.

H: Let's look at it objectively once more.

S: Yes, they—they're hungry.

H: Look at the rats!

S: Yes—

H: Do you like them—how do they look?

S: Black.

H: How is their fur?

S: Quite normal, but they have ugly tails.

H: What's so ugly about them?

S: They look so naked.

H: How do the tails look from an objective point of view?

S: They just have no fur—that's only—

H: Do you have fur all over your body?

S: Of course not, I'm a human—I have fairly long hair, but not all over my body.

H: Very well, what is objective about the tails?

S: Skin.

H: Yes, is that disgusting?

148—

S: In connection with the fur it looks ugly, you know—the fur is all right, but when you connect the naked tail with the fur—it doesn't look so pretty—that is—somehow it isn't esthetic, you know—if it had hair too, then I think . . .

H: Let's look at a rat's face—look at the head.

S: Well, that way they're actually sort of cute—but, well . . .

H: Now make up with the rats.

S: Okay.

H: But you must really mean it.

S: I really mean it.

H: That's good, they're really lovable and sweet little animals.

S: Well, I don't know if I'd call them lovable and sweet, but . . .

H: You have to learn to love their kind.

S: No, but you know, I understand now—you explained it to me. It's not the rats' fault.

H: Then you are angry with the people who let you starve?

S: Yes.

H: And you transferred this anger to the rats?

S: I did—yes.

H: Do you take back this anger?

S: Yes.

H: And you will give the rats the recognition they deserve?

S: Hm—give the rats recognition?

H: Well, you've already given it. It's okay. Let's go forward again to the year 1975.

S: Recognition, hm—

H: We shall now go forward to the year 1975—good—picture a rat in your mind.

S: Yes.

H: What sort of feeling do you get?

S: Nothing.

H: Everything okay?

S: Yes—it's simply a rat.

H: And a rat will never bother you again?

S: And what about my arm?

H: What's wrong with your arm?

S: I don't know.

H: Well, move it—you can move it. What's wrong with the arm?

S: I don't feel it.

H: Let's go back to the arm. Where did this arm originate? When did you get this lame arm?

S: 1812.

H: And what year is it now?

S: Mother's Day.

H: 1975.

S: Yes.

H: What is this lame arm doing in the year 1975?

S: Yes, but I——my God!

H: What's the matter?

S: But I'm—of course—I'm already dead.

H: This arm has no business in this life—it doesn't belong in this life—it's an aberration in time—we're living in the year 1975—and the arm feels fine.

S: Yes, I had forgotten that.

H: Good, move your arm.

S: Yes, it's fine.

H: You now have the opportunity of surveying your entire past. It is always ready to be reviewed by you—which does not mean that you should return to the past. We have done that once in order to make it known to you. You will always be fully conscious of it—but never forget—you are living in the here and now. The events from the past, those experiences, have nothing to do with the here and now—that is an anachronism—an aberration in time, if you continue to live with emotions dating back to days long gone by—and you will have the capability of immediately recognizing feelings that do not belong to the present as those that actually belong to the past; this will make you more and more aware every day. Your consciousness will become greater and deeper—you will be able to review your past completely—but you will realize that it is the past, that you are living in the here and now, completely in the present and not in the past with emotions attached to events of the long ago. Do you agree?

S: Yes.

H: And so all events of the past have lost their power over you because you know them, you recognize them—they have no further influence over you—because everything that is known has no influence—you have influence over what is known and not vice versa—only the unknown can have influence—and since the past is now fully known to you, it can do nothing to you— you are living entirely in the present—you are feeling well— do you feel this new well-being throughout your entire body?

S: My feet still hurt.

H: Where does this hurting of the feet belong?

S: 1725.

H: And what year are we in now?

S: 1975.

H: And how do your feet feel now?

S: Well, yes—I—you know, I keep forgetting—or I think I keep forgetting to simply leave it behind.

H: Let's leave the past behind us—where it belongs—we are living in the here and now—and in the now, you are feeling very well—you feel well, happy and satisfied—you have no problems— on the contrary—your entire body feels as if it's had a vacation— well rested and recuperated, as if you had been sleeping for hours, or even days—completely refreshed—can you feel that throughout your entire body? Do you feel it?

S: Yes.

H: Yes, really feel it—how does it feel?

S: Hm, not bad—comfortable, somehow.

H: All right—and now activity will return—you are active— you feel content and well—energy is flowing through your body; you feel well—you are now anxious to get going and do something, right?

S: Yes.

H: Now we shall bring this session to a conclusion—you will then be completely awake, and even in your waking state all the information you have gained in this session will be at your disposal—and you will feel very, very well.

The
Esoteric
and
Reincarnation

Even among otherwise intelligent people,
people who are well educated and with
considerable experience, one can occasionally
observe a virtual blindness, an almost systematic
anasthesia, when one attempts, for example,
to explain to them determinism.
C. G. JUNG

PYTHAGORAS IS SAID to have divided his lectures into two parts, namely, the esoteric teachings that were intended only for the inner circle of his school, and the exoteric teachings that were available even to those who were not actual members of his student body (esoteric is derived from the Greek esoteros = the inner, and is the opposite of exoteros = the outer). Since that time, the esoteric has become a collective concept for the secret teachings of initiates and has in this concept attracted so many questionable claims and speculations that it would seem to be almost daring to speak of "the esoteric." If I nevertheless persist in using this term, it is probably because in comparison to other available terminology, it arouses the least amount of prejudice. The esoteric to me means in its broadest sense the philosophical opposite of the monument known as natural science.

This polarization by no means indicates that both points of view must automatically always arrive at completely opposing results, conclusions, and views. The polarization is chiefly concerned with procedural techniques. In the final analysis, both have the same goal, namely, understanding the world, or more modestly expressed, a replica that as closely as possible represents reality. But opinions as to how this goal, which is as old as man himself, can best be attained, vary considerably and frequently depend on the fashion of the moment.

And so, for some generations man has thought along the lines of natural science and has connected this concept with a specific procedure. This procedure becomes a sort of measuring instrument with which one goes forth to measure "reality." This "measuring," taken literally this time, has become the highest criterion in natural science, because what you can measure must exist. The successes of the last few decades appear to attest to the accuracy of this procedure and this way of thinking.

This euphoria has become somewhat weakened in recent years as indicated by some warning hints from people who believe they clearly recognize the fact that with these successes new problems have arisen. The question remains whether we have come any closer to our goal of understanding the world and whether the individual as a "user" of this understanding can profit from it in the shaping of his life.

People do not like to hear this question or do not wish to understand it the way it is intended. We do not mean with this the many useful technical achievements that make it possible for man to cross unbelievable distances, to receive information from all over the world, and the like. The question that must be answered is aimed not at our modern conveniences or the pure increase in information, but at that which means being human. Today we have as many sick people as ever, and psychic illness increases with the rapidity of the suicide rate. Is modern man any happier? Obviously we do not have only sick and unhappy people, but did the happy ones get that way solely because of our technical achievements or our scientific flow of information? Is not our problem today due to this one-sided development? We have to thank natural science for an enormous development, but unfortunately this development was totally one-sided and concerned itself only with the purely functional part of reality.

Everything that manifests itself in the physical world contains two poles. Even the functional has an antipole. The content, the essential ingredient that cannot be measured in meters and grams, belongs to being human as much as the measurable and the material. Or to describe the difference between functionality and content more graphically: although Beethoven's Ninth Symphony can be physically dismembered and analyzed with measurable data such as frequency and phons, does this really measure that which makes "the Ninth" a true experience?

Many people are inclined to suspect that the opposite of rational, functional thinking is found in the field of faith or even superstition in which the door is open to each and every type of speculation. Faith may be the opposite of knowledge, but in this case it is not a decision between do I believe and do I know, but between the polarized functional knowledge and the knowledge that understands content.

The opportunity to achieve true, endowed knowledge, which is not only functional but allows an insight into content, has always existed and is today, the same as ever, used as the criterion for recognition.

This is the esoteric way, not exactly overcrowded with followers, but even here quantity should not be an indication of quality. The esoteric way has probably existed as long as there have been people who, in the search for the purpose of life, have not been afraid of making the effort to find the answer for themselves. Since this requires a special effort, it is not surprising that the esoteric way has never become a parade ground for the masses. But because of this, it has conquered time. By this, I mean that there is scarcely anything comparable that, like the esoteric, has remained completely independent of the spirit of the times, of the fashions, and of changes in opinion.

The esoteric does not age, because its theses are the laws of nature, of people and of life—all matters that remain the same regardless of the changes in their outward shape.

The esoteric strives for knowledge that does not become exhausted because of catalogued dates and formulas but that makes possible an understanding of the world and its laws. Since the esoteric cannot accept the world as something accidental and heterogeneous but considers it a cosmos in its true sense, it is possible to explore universal laws that are valid not only in one specific area but that can be found repeatedly as laws or principles on all levels on which they appear. The esoteric principle "like top, like bottom" (Hermes Trismegistos, Tabula smaragdina) permits, in analogy, a newly discovered law to be transferred to all levels of reality. Here one can clearly see the difference between the esoteric and the scientific procedure: while the esoteric works from the center to the periphery, physical science begins at the periphery and moves toward the center. Of course, it is still far removed from the center, because interdisciplinary agreement has become a big problem. The periphery corresponds to the diligent gathering of individual data, while the center represents the sought-after "world formula."

Another important difference between the esoteric and science is that in science one can take functional data and pass them on to others, take possession of them, or use them at will. This, unfortunately, cannot be done with the esoteric, since it does not depend so much on the collection of data as it does on personal understanding. And it is just as impossible to understand something for someone else as it is to eat or drink something for someone else. In the esoteric, everyone must do everything himself in order perhaps some day to become knowledgeable.

Whether this goal is worth striving for is something we shall have to determine at a later date. Here I shall first explain what I mean when I use the term "esoteric." In this connection, it may already have become clear that the esoteric and parapsychology can never be synonymous. Parapsychology is an offshoot of science and thinks functionally; that is, it collects, measures, and sorts out. Such occupation helps to fill up index-card boxes but not to develop a human being. For this reason, I consciously try to throw light on the reincarnation theme from the point of view of the esoteric in order to make it understandable, since I believe that in view of the highly scientific and technical developments of our time, we still have a great deal of catching up to do with regard to the development of our souls in order to be able to live together in internal as well as external harmony.

In the esoteric, reincarnation has always been an undisputed, foregone conclusion. The esoteric doctrine has for ages been aware of certain exercises and lessons with whose help and with long, diligent training, conscious reminiscence was made possible. In esoteric Buddhism, there is a stage of development that a person can only attain after he has consciously surveyed all his incarnations. A similar practice takes place in the schools of magic under the concept of "magical recollection." Aleister Crowley writes in his work *Magic as Philosophy for All, Book 4, Theory* about magical recollection, "There is no more important task than the study of our former incarnations." And relative to various techniques, he writes,

But the customary practice of Dharama is probably of greater general value. As soon as we keep the more easily accessible thoughts from surfacing, we come upon deeper layers. Recollections of childhood are reawakened. Another class of ideas whose origins might embarrass us lies even deeper. Some of them apparently belong to earlier incarnations. If we carefully tend these areas of our mind, we can develop them, we become more skillful, we create an orderly association out of previously disconnected elements, and our ability grows with surprising rapidity once we have mastered the tricks of the trade.

We see that recollection of previous incarnations is by no

means new. The only thing new, perhaps, is the "tricks of the trade" as Crowley calls the method that makes it possible to help someone obtain these recollections without years of training and meditation. This method, as a matter of fact, works so quickly and efficiently that I sometimes worry about whether it is really justifiable to catapult an individual into a state of conscious knowledge that he had no part in bringing about, simply because of a finely functioning technique. However, the esoteric principle that there is no such thing as chance helps to allay these fears. Looking at it from this point of view, I do not consider it mere chance when among billions of contemporaries, a few find their way to someone who makes these recollections possible for them.

The effect of becoming conscious of such matters depends for the most part on the conscious treatment of the material that has been brought to light and must for this reason always be handled by the individual himself. The law of polarity at this point permits a person to pay so little attention to the new recollections that slowly and effortlessly they can again disappear into the realm of the forgotten. This shows once more that not much can be obtained through simple functionality if we do not have the individual who is willing to struggle for understanding. Why this magic memory or reincarnation recollections are so important to esoteric training will be understood when we study the theory of reincarnation more closely.

Reincarnation is the law of periodicity. When we study nature, we observe everywhere a rhythm of appearing and disappearing, blooming and fading, day and night, summer and winter, life and death. In all of nature, there is no manifestation with a beginning and an ending, where the ending is not at the same time the beginning of something new, an antipode, just as there is no manifestation that does not have an antipode in its outward form. It is precisely this change in polarities that creates "living" in its broadest sense. An occurrence that has only a beginning and an ending would not fit into a whole such as our universe. How can a field be reversed when a matter is closed at both ends and cannot contain the rhythm of development? Only the cyclical happening creates the connection with the whole and becomes a union of polarized matters that encompasses both poles.

This cyclical happening can be seen everywhere in nature, whether it be the normal passing of a year, the tides of the sea, the periodic system of the elements, or the curve of electricity. The circle, or if we wish to consider its development, the spiral figure always reflects the principle of the living. In view of this undisputed fact, it seems to me as very daring to single out man himself as the exception to this regularity by postulating that human existence consists simply of being thrown into this rhythmic happening for a few decades without a before or hereafter.

This idea is neither logical nor obvious, but in one respect it is very practical: it relieves man of all responsibility. After all, if there is nothing but the short stretch between life and death, he can safely do or not do whatever he wants; he will make his rounds until the end of his life and "after me, the deluge."

It is easy to understand why many people are irritated and angry when one speaks of reincarnation, because suddenly they find responsibility thrust upon them from two sides, a before and a hereafter that throw an entirely different light on the "now." Suddenly this thought cuts off all means of escape, because where is one to flee if one constantly keeps meeting one's self? It must be a shock for all who believe that suicide or, expressed more nobly, freedom of death, will be their last willful act on earth. But here again we find polarity: eliminate responsibility and life loses its meaning.

There is scarcely a question that is as embarrassing to people as asking them, "What is your aim in life?" At first, one might hear a few self-conscious phrases such as happiness, contentment, family, children, perhaps even diligence, love of fellow man, and the like. Then if one digs deeper, one comes upon a void that must be the foundation of a life that wants to know nothing of a union with or a responsibility toward the cosmos. Here one notices the close connection between the crisis of a human being that one tends to call a neurosis and the crisis of a system of thinking that attempts to release man within its functionality. Thus we see two alternatives, life with meaning and responsibility or life with neither.

I know that to ask life's meaning in the world of today may sound antiquated because it makes one think of a "healthy world" and disturbs all those who want to make dissatisfaction, conflicts, and unsolvable problems into world principles. These people don't want anything "healthy." Only fools and simpletons still find something healthy; if you wish to be an intellectual, you must live with foolishness. In view of this simplification, it would seem more worthwhile sometimes to be considered among the fools than to represent professional pessimism.

If one were to ask why some people have such great hatred for the healthy world or of the thought systems that emphasize the meaning of life, I suspect that the answer would be that they are trying desperately to hide their own despair and inner emptiness. Let us therefore not be disturbed by those who look at us sympathetically with a knowing wink and who benevolently offer the comment that "all this smacks very much of a do-it-yourself healthy-world concept, a little too fearless to be taken seriously."

Let us assume that we have decided that life requires responsibility as well as meaning. The question thereupon arises as to how both can be realized in one life between birth and death. Even the most serious decision to live responsibly must be able to answer the question, responsible to whom or to what? A system of values is required, but the yardsticks of values are of variable length. The search for meaning is even more difficult. Where is the meaning of the life of a human being that is snuffed out after only twenty years? Where is the meaning in a blind or crippled person, in a poor or a rich man? Fate is the answer, but who is to tell us the meaning of fate?

We go around in circles when it comes to these questions, even when we take into consideration the official version of the Christian church. The simple system of punishment and salvation is far from being an answer to why certain persons suffer certain fates, why fates can vary so greatly, and why "new souls" are constantly exposed to a bodily existence for a few years, only to be consigned thereafter either to salvation or damnation. This model is not more meaningful than the materialistic one, except that the aspect of responsibility is strengthened by the fear of punishment.

Going back to the idea of reincarnation, we shall see that all open questions will find an answer and produce a meaningful whole. It seems important to me that regardless of any functional indicators as to whether or not there is such a thing as reincarnation, it is clearly recognized that likelihood is unequivocally on the side of reincarnation. It would be most surprising if it could be proven that there is no rebirth. Strangely enough, many people turn this situation around and consider reincarnation as most unlikely, for which reason, in their opinion, especially strict criteria must be used in any possible demonstration. These people, however, confuse "unlikely" with "unaccustomed." If one has believed long enough that the atom can't be split, one is unaccustomed to the opposite, but it is by no means unlikely.

Experience teaches us that everything we observe shows development and is involved in evolution. I use the concept of evolution not as Darwin did, as one of chance and a development based on survival. The evolution in my theory is exactly the opposite of chance; it is regularity and a plan of higher development. There is no chance. We live in a cosmos that, translated literally, means "orderly." This cosmos depends on everything going according to a plan; every deviation therefrom is a disturbance of the entirety and therefore a danger for the whole. A cosmos with room for coincidence or chance is a contradiction in itself.

All of natural science depends on this regularity. No one seriously believes that a stone that we drop might suddenly fly up into the sky or that the moon might leave its orbit and disappear in the direction of Saturn simply because it experiences a desire to do so. Only man is granted the freedom to do or not do what he wants, but he too is embedded in this regularity. Yes, even the law of probability demonstrates that over and above coincidence or chance there is a law that evens out all chance over a given period of time. We must decide whether we recognize a cosmos with regularity or a chaos with chance. Under no circumstances is there a mixture of the two, for example, a cosmos with chance. Since on the basis of our observations and experience we all have reason to believe in a cosmos, we should consequently strike the idea of chance out of our thinking completely. This will also prevent our believing in the possibility that a chance development, evoked by the mutation of a few genes, which by virtue of a timely coincidence might create a human out of an eggwhite molecule.

Evolution in our frame of reference is intentional higher development, a law that is effective throughout the universe and that encompasses all creation. Man as a part of this whole, as a wheel in this inconceivable clockwork, must obey this law of development because the whole can only develop when all of its parts develop. Man's task therefore is development and nothing else! Development, however, does not occur by itself, but is always the product of energetic discussion, a product of the learning process. In order to learn, one needs a problem, because only through trial and error can one reach a solution; only by solving problems can one learn, and only by learning can one develop.

Fate is the collective concept for the many problems that beset man in the course of his life in order to present him with the necessary ingredients for his development. Problems are the lessons from which he must learn. Problems are not something negative as is erroneously believed by some, but an aid in the development of the individual in his fulfillment and in his evolution.

On the basis of the law of polarity, however, man has two ways of learning, the active and the passive way. To learn actively means to face each problem happily and to consider it an invitation to learning in order to get a step higher in one's personal development. Unfortunately, only a minority seeks this learning process. Much more frequently we attempt to avoid the problem, to sidestep it, and to suppress it. In such a case, the individual, by virtue of an unconscious wish, is manipulated into a situation in which he learns passively what he tried to avoid learning actively.

This passive situation is always connected with suffering. Such a situation is called "a stroke of fate," "sickness," or "an accident." One complains and feels that he has been treated unjustly. However, on the outside there are no guilty individuals; not people, not the surrounding world, not fate nor God. The only one at fault is the sufferer himself, for he had a choice—although not through free will, as is frequently claimed—the choice of active or passive learning. The law does not allow "not learning," for this would be stagnation and would be damaging to all development. The much praised "free will" is limited to a "free choice" that always leads to a learning process, a little bit of development. Free will would permit varying results; this contradicts the regularity of a cosmos. The "choice," however, is a product of the laws of polarity and does not endanger orderly development.

Fate is anything but an anonymous, unfathomable power that threatens man by its coincidence and caprice. Fate is something extremely personal, the result of one's own doing, the regular auxiliary of evolution. This truth is uncomfortable for those who have become accustomed to blaming their fate on the outside world and thus shedding all responsibility. These people react so violently and so emotionally to the esoteric because they feel their living lie threatened. However, it is they who need truth most urgently in order to free themselves from their own error.

They constantly hope for and request help from the outside, from others. This hope is absurd. Others, even physicians and therapists, can only lend functional assistance, but this assistance solves no problems because all those who call for help, in the final analysis, suffer because they could not solve their problems and did not want to learn. Can outsiders help them? This is just as impossible as asking someone to eat for me or go to the bathroom for me. There are certain things that one must do himself, and development is one of the first of these.

This concept of individual evolution cannot be applied to a person who possesses only one single corporal life, since the point of departure, suppositions, and stipulations of a life are too varied. If we separate the individuality of a human being, or his consciousness, from his material appearance, we will realize that this "id" will develop cyclically into a higher stage through a chain of reembodiments toward the goal of perfection.

Now the differences in the fate of various human beings can be understood because each is in a different specific stage of development and in order to advance needs specific problems and experiences. The fate of this life is therefore a result of the previous "chain of lives," a consequence of what was previously learned or not learned. Everyone at times goes through those problems that he did not conquer in the past through conscious learning, and in the future he will again be confronted with one and the same problem until he has solved it for himself.

This regularity is known by the Indian name of "karma," and "karma" requires that a problem be experienced continuously until it is understood. This law is independent of time. The cosmos requires that regularity be observed, but it is completely unimportant whether someone requires thirty or three thousand years for the learning process, because time coordinates exist only in our consciousness and not in reality.

The idea is generally very difficult for man to understand. Our thinking is so firmly bound to our measurement of time that we forget how "human" this measurement of time is and that it can make no claims on absolutism. Every system, every species of life has "its time." Time is something relative. We know this from our dreams. In a period of a few seconds, we can have a dream whose time extends over a number of years. Our measurement of time is valid only for us human beings and only for as long as we possess consciousness. A fly that lives only one day, for example, lives just as long as a human who gets to be eighty years old, because it exists in a different relative time. Reality knows no time; we humans and the other forms of life, however, are forced to experience reality within a time continuum.

The following example will illustrate this. In Munich there is a large museum with, let us say, thirty rooms. The director of this museum knows all thirty rooms inside and out as do the guards and some of the frequent visitors. They have all known for years how every room looks, what is in it, and how it is furnished. Now let us assume that I know nothing about this museum at the present time but have decided to visit it tomorrow morning at ten o'clock. If, for example, while viewing it, I have arrived in room number three at 10:30 A.M., I know what is in these rooms, but I do not know what is to be seen in the remaining twenty-seven rooms. I will only know that when I have also been in them. I can, however, only do that within the time coordinate. Time will pass until I get to see room twenty-eight. This fact, though, must not induce me to conclude that during the time I am in room three, rooms four to thirty do not exist and will only come into being when I enter them. My entire personal knowledge of these rooms is dependent on time; I cannot get to know the rooms without loss of time. Of course, I can perhaps thumb through the museum catalog while in room three and look at some pictures of the other rooms, but this information will not replace "having been there."

If we transpose this example to our life and experiences, the time concept becomes clear. Reality exists independent of the passing of time, similar to our museum. Man, however, can only see and experience this reality within a time coordinate, but he must not conclude from this that what he is seeing and experiencing is just coming into existence at this moment. Reality is timeless and omnipresent, but we cannot recognize it that way. It is a thick book that we are holding in our hands but have not yet read. In order to know what is in it, we must start on page one and read it page by page. Time will pass while doing this. Nevertheless, the contents of the book have existed from the start, regardless of how much time it took to read it: Next year, with all its events, is equally independent of time and has always existed, but we will have to wait until we can see it and participate in it.

The person who can understand this will also be able to understand how clairvoyance and precognition came into being. Knowing in advance about a future happening is like thumbing through the catalog during our museum visit in order to learn about what has not yet been experienced. The seeing of scenes from the future, which is called precognition, is spontaneously possible for some individuals, but it can also be learned and can be produced experimentally. This look into the future, however, is only a viewing and is not a substitute for experiencing the same thing. Even if one knows today what will happen tomorrow, it cannot be experienced until tomorrow. But all those who expect an enormous personal advantage from their "look into the future" (usually the first request is with regard to lottery numbers!) have not grasped the concept of time.

Precognition of the future is possible precisely because the future happening already exists in reality and not, as we imagine, is only going to happen. This excludes all possibility of personal steering or influence on the future. Most people do not want to admit this, especially when they are proud of their activity with which they believe they can shape the future. Here the word "believe" must be emphasized. Spinoza said, "If the thrown stone possessed consciousness, it would believe it could fly because it wanted to!"

Man possesses only one freedom, namely, to believe that he is free. Everything else happens as ordained. It happens and man says, "I did it." One thing left to man, however, is choice. Since reality reveals itself to man in polarized fashion, this polarization offers man a possibility of choice. He can choose how he wishes to observe the law of regularity, but observe it he must. This thought of predetermination seems to be unbearable to many: they scornfully call it "fatalism." This reaction, of course, indicates that determinism was not understood. Determinism does not in anyway lead to resignation, but on the contrary, leads to complete freedom from fear, an understanding of the significance of life, and, yes, to freedom itself. This freedom is the quintessence of the following four steps:

1. Complete knowledge of oneself.
2. Complete knowledge of the law.
3. Acceptance of the natural order of things as necessary and good.
4. Voluntary submission to the natural order of things.

The person who takes these four steps will see a paradox: he will be free! This freedom, however, is completely different from what the person who thinks he is free considers to be freedom. The latter, because of his procedure based on his erroneous belief in his freedom of action, constantly contradicts the existing law, which is not understood by him.

He is like a person who tries to do something impossible because he does not know it is impossible. A necessary discrepancy almost always exists between procedure and reality. Since reality must correct erroneous procedure in order to maintain itself, suffering results, for suffering is the result of ignorance.

But he who knows himself, his talents, his tasks, his needs, and his stage of development and beyond this recognizes the cosmic laws and voluntarily submits himself to them will live in harmony with reality. He permits no distinction between what is to be and what he would like. Christianity expresses this procedure with the words, "Thy will be done." It is only this person who is actually free, free of all unpleasantness that is caused by the difference between the law and his own desires. Christianity calls this difference a "sin," the separation from reality. Aleister Crowley, in his work *Magic, Book 4*, also speaks of this when he says, "The best oath . . . is the oath of holy obedience because it does not lead to complete freedom, but is a form of training in submission, which is the final lesson."

We can see that only when we give up the illusion of freedom does a path open up that leads to freedom. This may sound like a paradox, but every truth must be a paradox because it embraces polarity. Free will is nothing more than "the effort to create a confluence of our secular will into the immutable· will or the highest law—into the moral law above me or within me" (Adler). In order to attain this confluence, man must wrestle with his fate, must learn and mature, must become conscious of his inner self. To learn all this, there is a school—the "school of life."

"Life" here is not to be equated with a specific corporal existence, but refers to the continuum "life" that rhythmically materializes with or without a body. This analogy between life and school will be used to further explain the concept of reincarnation.

Let us imagine a school with many classes, a fixed curriculum, and a well-defined educational goal. The school represents humanity, the individual classes represent the various stages of development of the soul, the material to be learned represents fate, and the educational goal is the perfection of man. This concept of perfection may irritate some and appear hybrid to them. But perfection here refers exclusively to the human domain. This human domain is a plane, a stratum in the enormous hierarchy of living creatures that are not human. Perfection always refers only to that level to which a living being belongs at a particular time. The goal of man is to become a perfect human being. He who considers this presumptuous or perhaps even blasphemous need only refer to Christ's sermon on the mount (Matthew 5:48): "Therefore be ye perfect as your Heavenly Father is perfect."

This perfection is the educational goal of our "school of life." When one starts school, he is far removed from his final goal. To reach it, he must begin in the lowest grade. There are problems for the student to solve, and he works these to the best of his ability. If he makes mistakes, he will get additional problems and lessons until he understands the principle to be learned. Only then can he proceed a step further.

The analogy with man is clear. He tries to overcome his problems and is presented with the same problems over and over until he has learned a specific principle of the cosmos. As soon as he has learned this, he is faced with the next problem, the next step.

In school, there will at some time be a major examination. Here the student will again try to do his best; he will get many things right but will also make many mistakes. He turns in his paper and leaves the classroom. In the hall, he receives a paper with the answers. Now he sees at a glance what he did right and what he did wrong, but it cannot help him now. He may be angry, he may wish to take the examination over with his newly acquired knowledge, but now he can do nothing with this knowledge obtained from the answer sheet. His time is up. He must wait for a new examination to use this knowledge—assuming he remembers it that long.

This examination situation, which is familiar to everyone, is the life of man within the concept of a material incarnation. He tries to solve his problems. Leaving the classroom is death—and here something truly unusual occurs.

After consciousness has left the body, this being (now without a body) stands before an absolute power in whose presence he instantly recognizes the mistakes he made in his life. He finds himself within a new system of values that represents a model of reality that, contrary to our polarity principle, makes it possible to immediately recognize clearly any deviation therefrom. One might compare this procedure with a stencil that is placed over our life so that with one glance we can recognize all correct and incorrect answers.

Of course, if we use concepts such as "right" and "wrong,"

"good" and "bad" in judging a human life, the question arises as to the point of reference. We humans almost always deal with concepts of value that refer to some system of morals. Nature dose not recognize a valuation in this sense. There is no "good" or "bad," because good and bad, to use these concepts as an example, are the polarized aspects of one and the same reality. If, therefore, we ask for the point of reference on the basis of which man, after he dies, recognizes the mistakes made in his life, one might best describe this polarity as "legal" and "illegal." If we find a defective transistor inside a computer, we do not change it because it is bad and we want to punish it, but because it prevents the proper functioning of the entire system. Nature works in a similar manner. It does not evaluate, does not reward, and does not punish. It sees to it, however, that development is permitted to take place without interruption.

It is obvious that the results of a person's behavior vary, depending on whether he lives in conformance with the law or opposes it. These varying results will be experienced by him as reward or punishment, but this experience is a purely subjective happening in the individual himself.

To live right means to live within the law. We are therefore not dealing with the development of a theory or the support of a particular religion or philosophy. On the contrary, I am describing here the results of a number of experiments in which all participating subjects described the same impressions and the same associations in spite of the fact that they represented quite a variety of philosophies and knew nothing of what other subjects had said. It is remarkable how many statements made during the sessions, especially those dealing with experiences after death, had strong religious overtones and reminded one of the Ten Commandments. Even more noteworthy was the fact that this was the case with admitted atheists as well as religiously oriented persons. The stories told by subjects under hypnosis had a great deal in common in spite of their varied education, philosophy, and ages. From this one can conclude that the various religions must have attempted, each in its own way, to offer man this basic precept or reality as an aid in the form of commandments.

Even should the individual during his stay on earth be torn between belief and disbelief in these commandments, he will, no later than the day of his death, come face to face with reality and know what he should or should not have done in order to obey the laws of the world. In this stage, there is neither faith nor doubt, only an obvious recognition of reality. In this after-death condition, there are no emotional evaluations. The individual has discovered the distance between this and his earthly life.

This distance now makes it possible to view earthly matters as a whole, without polar fixations. But as long as we try to evaluate, we are in a state of fixation and cannot see the whole. Through his release from the body, man releases himself from his ties and looks over his past life. And with the recognition of his shortcomings, he recognizes at the same time the need to learn more. This, however, he can only do in another earthly life and with a body. He realizes that he must return to earth and begin another corporal existence.

It is actually experienced as a "must" and not, as we might assume, a favor. It may sound surprising to hear that all subjects, without exception, were so happy and satisfied with their condition after death that no one had the desire to return to a corporal existence but reluctantly agreed that they would "unfortunately" have to lead another life in order to continue their development. It seems ironic that most people on earth want to cling to their earthly existence with all their might, while all those on the other side of life look forward to their new corporal existence with just as much fear.

The living human has a burning desire to know how things look in "the hereafter," "the realm of the dead," or "the other side." The "other side" is the opposite of "this side." It is the other, the opposite, which complements "this side." Both together form a unit. The one could not exist without the other. This side and the other side are two aspects of one and the same reality. Since in the final analysis they are one unit, they do not vary on a scale of values, nor are they different levels in a hierarchy. Those on the other side are neither higher nor lower than people here on earth. Dying is no more a step forward than it is a step backward. Dying is only a change to the other polarity.

In the vernacular, sleep is called the little brother of death. This comparison fits the situation exactly. Waking and sleeping are the same, but smaller, rhythm as life and death (actually it should be called living with and without a body.) We know that sleep combined with its dream function is an occurrence important to life. One can be awake for some time, but then one sleeps. If this rhythmic change is withdrawn from a person, physical death may occur, because sleep and dreams have important balancing functions to perform in one's daily life.

The same thing happens in a rhythmic change of life and death. The condition after death is like a dream, a processing phase of life. Only the overview of a life and the confrontation with reality will make possible the further development of man and will prevent him from getting hopelessly lost in a maze of errors. It is precisely these parallel happenings such as waking and sleeping and life and death that indicate only too clearly how sensible and logical the idea of reincarnation is, even without the experimental proof.

It is a sad state of affairs when a culture has so little understanding of legal procedures and similar matters that it demands functional "proof" for the simplest and most natural happenings. We find the same laws everywhere in the world—discernible only by their difference in scope. This recognition of a principle on different levels is the strength of the hermetic philosophy: "That which is below is the same as that which is above," or in the view of Paracelsus: The macrocosm corresponds to the microcosm.

This view of the whole has unfortunately been lost more and more frequently, due to scientific specialization. Many would rather believe statistics than dare to open their eyes in order to see and understand. From mathematics and the technical world, we know the so-called sine curve. It is the graphic model of all phenomena that expire cyclically in the real world. It reflects a law of nature. This sine curve also represents the pattern of reincarnation. Every crossing of the axis from the positive to the negative and vice versa is a turning point in a reversal of polarity. In our case, the crossing represents conception and death, entry into matter and exit from the corporal.

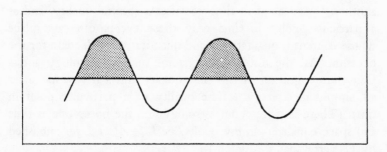

Here the question arises as to the timing of the axis crossing. We have previously discussed the relativity and subjectivity of time. Every system in the universe has its time. The animal lives in a different time period from the human. Even in the life of a human, the time experience changes as he gets older. If a year seems an eternity for a child, this year shrinks more and more in the life of an adult and gets shorter, the older he gets. (Only at a greatly advanced age is this experience reversed again.)

The difference in time experience comes even clearer with reference to other life forms. A fly that lives only one day, as we have said previously, lives just as long as an eighty-year-old human, because the fly does not live in our time, but in its own time system. We must be aware of this subjectivity in our concept of time when we ask about the time frame of reincarnation. We can count the individual segments only with our time scale, although it is not valid for the noncorporal period of life. After death, there is no concept of time in our sense. The closest comparison we can make is that it is the same as our sense of time while we are asleep. Without external orientation, we cannot tell upon awakening how long we slept. This phenomenon also appears in hypnosis.

When we speak of time, we usually refer to "duration." We pay far too little attention to the other aspect of time, namely, its qualitative content. The quality of time is particularly interesting, since the various time systems seem to combine with one another. Every point in time possesses a specific quality, and at a particular point in time only those events can take place whose content is qualitatively and quantitatively adequate for the occasion. All the old mantic systems such as astrology and I Ching are cognizant of this time quality and a horoscope, after all, simply illustrates the time quality of a particular point in time. (There is more about astrology and the horoscope as time and space equalizers in my book *The Life After Life*, published by C. Bertelsmann, Munich.)

This time quality is the deciding factor in conception, birth, and death. In order to understand it better, let us examine the law of contents and form. Everyone by his thoughts and deeds puts contents into the world and must redeem them by experiencing them. This is a different definition for what we previously called responsibility. Contents and form together create a closed learning cycle. Fate is the formal happening as an expression of the established contents. Thus, during his life, man constantly redeems his own contents. When he dies, a large part of the contents remains unredeemed; there is a great deal of remaining stock—the learning cycles that are not yet closed and the realities that are not yet understood.

This learning deficit that man takes with him to the after-death state is what determines his fate during the next life. Imagine that at the end of an earthly life there is a balance such as that in the books of a corporation at the end of a year. If you think of this final balance as a sort of code number, the soul will remain in the after-death state until a point in time arrives that contains a quality that corresponds to the quality of this code number. When time quality and soul contents match, this affinity will effect a new connection with matter, and what we call conception takes place.

These periods between individual incarnations when measured by our system of time can be of varying duration. According to experience gained from my experiments, they can vary from several hundred years to a few decades. It is an old esoteric assertion that the maturity of a soul is correlated with the length of time intervals. The less mature the soul, the sooner the next incarnation. I have been unable to determine in my experiments whether this rule is valid, but it appears to be self-evident. It is quite conceivable that a great discrepancy between the way of life has been lived and the reality model presents a strong need for new embodiment.

I can confirm one other claim, which is that time intervals between incarnations are especially brief at present. It is a fact that the further back I go with my subjects, the longer the time intervals become. This is illogical with reference to the first hypothesis, since as a result of constantly growing maturity, one can expect constantly increasing time intervals. This question must remain unanswered for the time being.

But this theme brings us to the argument most frequently used against the idea of reincarnation. Rebirth does not make sense in view of the tremendous growth in population. To me, however, the population explosion does not appear to be a valid argument against reincarnation because by shortening or lengthening the time intervals between incarnations, the population size at any given moment can be controlled at will. The above-mentioned experience, the fact that at present the time intervals are very short, also points in this direction. Apparently, two natural laws overlap here, one pertaining to the individual, the other impersonal. My assistants at present are verifying the sequence of incarnation dates in accordance with astrological points of view in the hope of obtaining more information about these laws.

The question of population increase brings up another problem: Where do the souls come from and where do they go? Here we must first clear away an old and deeply rooted prejudice that quietly insists that except for humans and perhaps animals, there are no living creatures with souls. This assumption appears to the human to be easy to verify since he starts with the premise that any other form of life must naturally look just like man. But this is exactly the reason for the false conclusion. If a bacterium were to start with the premise that everything that is alive must look and act like a bacterium, it could never recognize the existence of man.

This intellectual error on the part of man was beautifully and appropriately caricatured by Egon Friedell in his short story, "Is There Life on Earth?" Friedell describes how the learned men of the innermost planet of the Cygnus constellation were studying the question as to whether the satellites of the sun contained life or at least had life-sustaining possibilities. This question was unanimously answered in the negative because their scientific knowledge of the planet Earth proved that life thereon was completely impossible. This decision, of course, is based on the Cygnotic scientists' knowledge of themselves. They are, as everyone knows, floating aerial beings who feed on light and who require a minimum temperature of far more than 500 degrees Centigrade. Only one unsalaried university lecturer in philosophy dares to contradict them and states, "Naturally all solar planets contain life, as do all heavenly bodies. A dead star would be a contradiction in itself. Every heavenly body represents a step toward perfection, each a degree nearer to spiritualization. Each is a thought of God's; therefore it lives and contains life, even if its inhabitants do not look like a Cygnotic professor of astronomy." As punishment for mocking the faculty, his thought transference permit was revoked.

Unfortunately such an intellectual reversal of the usual stream of thought is difficult not only for the Cygnots in Friedell's story but also for many people on our planet. We should nevertheless get away from the idea that we humans are the focal point of the universe. We humans belong to a specific kingdom of nature, namely, the human race. This human race is a small group in the giant hierarchy of living beings. Above and below us humans are a large number of such "kingdoms" that in their present form are completely different from human beings, but nevertheless exist, are alive, and have souls. They too are members of the evolution of the universe, and they too learn how to grow to higher levels.

When I first spoke of perfection, I emphasized "with reference to humans," for every living being develops in the direction of "its own" perfection, the perfection pertaining to its own domain. This is valid for the plant as well as for the animal and for all other living creatures not as well known. Once an individual has attained perfection within his own group, he is able to move into the next higher rank in the hierarchy and continue his development there. Thus every level is a passageway with an entrance and an exit. On one side, there is a streaming-in from a lower level, while on the other side, those who have attained "perfection" move up to the next level in the hierarchy. Since the human race is such a passageway, there is no need to play with numbers so as to guess how many souls it all started with and how they multiplied.

At the same time, this pattern presents another interesting aspect. If the human race were a closed community and we believed in a higher development, the "world" would have to improve constantly until it consisted completely of perfect people. The world, however, will not change materially when it comes to the distribution of understanding because it represents only one segment of development. It is similar to a class in school—the third grade will never get any smarter because those who have learned leave it and others take their place.

I know that even this concept of the hierarchy of living creatures will appear unfamiliar to many, but before it is pushed aside with a smile, we should think about how obvious we consider this hierarchy concept in other areas, for example, in the periodic law of the elements. Furthermore, this concept is not a speculation, but can be experienced by humans—provided they are prepared for such an experience. Thus, for example, spiritualism provides ways and means of becoming aware of beings on another plane. We must remember, though, that he who does not want to see, will not see.

In connection with the subject of immortality and reincarnation, we often hear such questions as "Will you see the dead again?" "Can I contact them?" "Will I meet them in the next world?" A great deal of sentimentality attaches to these questions, which are formulated from the point of view of the living. The so-called dead person does not in any way share the sentimentality and sorrow of the bereaved. Death in lightning-like fashion cuts away from all earthly events and thus excludes any and all emotion. It is in this new existence that man learns to view all reality without any polar fixation. Emotion is created only by fixation. The deceased does not mourn those he has left behind. He finds himself in a new environment with new problems, outside the realm of love and hatred. Here, too, we see the similarity to sleep, which erases and dissolves many an emotion of the day.

The question of reunion on the other side arises from the usual manner of projecting "this side" on the "other side." For many, that "other side" is of better quality than "this side." Here one overlooks the fact that we are dealing with an antipole that of necessity is completely different and not simply an improvement on a known factor. There is no reunion on the other side and no contact between the departed with one another.

Spiritualists are of a different opinion, but perhaps this is only a misunderstanding. Spiritualists are in contact with some sort of spirits who may or may not be humans waiting for reincarnation. Here we might actually already be dealing with another hierarchy. At any rate, no one has ever told me of any sort of contact with other beings; questions to that effect have always been answered in the negative.

This refers to contact with beings on the same level. The possibility of contacting the living, however, has been answered affirmatively. Such contact, though, must be made by the living, because the "dead" lack adequate means of making themselves known to humans, because the dead lack the necessary sensitivity.

Whether such a contact between living and dead is of any value is questionable. The person who looks at death from the proper point of view will permit his relative, no matter how beloved, to enter the new domain without attempting any type of contact. This is particularly important to the act of dying itself. One must not make the mistake of calling back the dying, since this might make the transition more difficult.

This remark will automatically reveal my attitude toward the methods of modern medicine that would by force revive the dead and unfortunately sometimes do. The levels on this side and the other side are so varied that communication is actually of no value. If anyone feels strongly enough that he must still say something to the deceased, this should be done within a few days after death. At first, the departed remains in the vicinity of his body and still possesses all his faculties. This does not mean, however, that one ought to try to pin down the dead. After all, we let the sleeping sleep and do not disturb their dreams.

With regard to a reunion in the great beyond, there is no such thing. The other side is not a place where souls walk around waiting happily to shake hands with every newcomer. After death, the deceased possess a pure consciousness that is virtually unimaginable for a human being. If you try to imagine what it is like to be a particular light wave of a television program, you will probably come close to reality. The individual who is well versed in meditation may also be able to picture what it is like to be a consciousness without a body. In this condition, one may still be able to perceive the happenings on earth, but after a few days the deceased will remove himself from these impressions and soon lose interest in them.

There can nevertheless be a reunion with the dead, not on the other side, but somewhere on earth at some other time, because humans will continue to make contact with the same people as long as they have mutual problems to solve. Ever since I chanced by accident upon this law of nature, I have tried at every session to observe which people repeatedly appear in the various lives. This frequently results in the most unusual surprises.

These factors also throw more light on the Oedipus and Electra complexes, because I have been able to determine in numerous cases that married couples or lovers in earlier lives have returned in a father-daughter or mother-son relationship. Here, too, many people will wrongly argue that the prior life was a projection of the Oedipus complex. As I have shown previously, I believe I am well able to determine the difference between projection and recollection of prior lives. I believe that stories concerning people who lived through several incarnations together are just as factual and can be substantiated just as well as other statements. In this connection, it is noteworthy that the sex remains the same throughout many incarnations and that a change from male to female and vice versa takes place in larger cycles. This is purely a discovery resulting from my experiments—I know no reason for it.

In conclusion, one question remains. What importance can be attached to these reincarnation experiments from an esoteric viewpoint? There are two aspects to this. In the first place, these experiments offer the experimenter tremendous insight into and information concerning procedures that hitherto were almost completely closed to any experimental attempts. We have become familiar with principles and ideas that were previously either unknown or, at best, known only to certain mediums or initiates. These, of course, were the reasons I began these experiments about ten years ago.

In the meantime, however, results have been achieved that affect the subject much more than the experimenter. Since we have made the contents of our sessions fully known to the subjects, their experiences have developed by themselves. Whereas I was originally afraid of such consequences, my experience since then has taught me just the opposite. The knowledge of former incarnations effects an enormous increase in a person's conscious knowledge. The individual suddenly learns how to interpret and understand details of his present life in a new manner; he recognizes associations and receives insights that greatly expedite his learning process. In the case of some subjects with whom we worked for about a year, we were able to observe tremendous changes in personality that were confirmed not only by the subjects themselves but also by their families, without exception.

These results can be explained as follows: Man does not recognize reality, because he looks at everything through the "lenses" of his previous learning experience. Everything he observes, therefore, is in some way emotionally charged. Let us illustrate:

If in 1493 someone burned to death in his house, it is still impossible for him today to observe fire without emotion and without prejudice, because every fire, every burning house, restimulates in his subconscious his 500-year-old fears. Although the incident itself may be suppressed, he projects his feelings onto the current event. Man for this reason never lives completely in the present, but always a little bit in the past.

If these experiences from earlier years are made known to him, this filter immediately disappears, and he is able to see reality as it is now, without confusing it with feelings from the distant past. Thus, becoming acquainted with one's former lives is by no means a flight into the past, but actually a prerequisite to separating the past from the present. This process makes possible what wise men constantly demand but is so difficult to do, namely, to live always, completely, and consciously in the present. Becoming conscious of one's incarnations will lead to this goal. For this reason, our reincarnation experiments have become, in addition to their therapeutic use, a means of esoteric education and a path to self-fulfillment.

The Natasha Case

First Session

S: I am cold.

H: Why are you cold?

S: I don't know. I should not have gone out.

H: Out where?

S: Out of the palace and . . .

H: Why not?

S: Because my father is scolding me now and because everyone who saw me is getting a beating.

H: What is he saying?

S: I didn't—oh, I'm so cold.

H: What is he saying?

S: I should not have left.

H: Left from where?

S: From my room.

H: Why not?

S: Because he is afraid something will happen to me.

H: Is it that bad?

S: Yes.

H: Can you explain that more clearly?

S: He said there is unrest and that is why [*moans*].

H: Why?

S: He is afraid for us.

H: How old are you?

S: I am twelve.

H: Do you have brothers or sisters?

S: Yes.

H: How many?

S: One is sick.

H: Your sister?

S: Now he is taking my hand and threatening me.

H: Yes, how?

S: Everyone is being punished because I was outside.

H: And you are afraid?

S: Yes. Oh, my God, what is it now?

H: What is happening? Tell me what is going on.

S: We are going into a very large room.

H: And what is there? What is in the room?

S: A beautiful woman is sitting there at a long table.

H: Who is this woman?

S: That must be my mother.

H: What is so bad about that?

S: Because I feel the cold.

H: What cold?

S: Everything feels cold.

H: Where is the cold coming from?

S: My mother is not kind to me. She is not warm—only beautiful. She has dark hair, combed away from her face—she has a lace scarf over her head and she is very pale. Why am I here?

H: Why does that surprise you?

S: She is unbelievably beautiful. I know she has—she is always pulling on my dress. I am wearing an ankle-length dress with lots of brocade and lace on the puffed sleeves—she is always pulling on them. I don't like her to touch me.

H: What is the matter?

S: [*Moans softly*]

H: You dislike her touching you so much?

S: Yes.

H: Is there anything else you don't like?

S: The unending, these . . . these halls. I always, I am always afraid . . .

H: You don't like it here?

S: No, no!

H: What is your name?

S: Natasha.

H: What is that?

S: Natasha, no, they call me Natasha, but it's not my name. My name is different, but I don't like it. That one who is always with me, she always calls me Natasha.

H: What is your name?

S: And then my mother scolds her.

H: And what does your mother call you?

S: "Child," that's all. She only says "child," because she knows that . . .

H: What sort of name is that, that you don't like?

S: She only calls me "child."

H: You don't like your name?

S: No.

H: What is it, anyway?

S: No.

H: Why no?

S: I don't like it.

H: What is it that you don't like?

S: Oh, no.

H: Is it that bad?

S: Yes.

H: Tell me anyway.

S: [*Sighs*]

H: Surely you can tell it to me just once.

S: No, no, I don't want to!

H: Say it quickly. Tell me the name.

S: [*Cries*].

H: Don't you want to say it?

S: No.

H: Why does this bother you? Don't you like it? Are you connecting it with some recollection? What is the reason that you don't want to tell me?

S: I am bad.

H: Please.

S: No.

H: Why are you bad?

S: I don't want anyone to know my name.

H: Why not?

S: Because I am bad.

H: Why are you bad?

S: I am cruel and . . .

H: What is this? Why are you cruel, and what are you doing that's cruel?

S: Hm.

H: What are you doing that is so cruel? You can tell me!

S: My mother is going to the window with me. It is a high, narrow window with Roman arches up on top.

H: What is the matter?

S: The Czar, what is the matter with the Czar?

H: I beg your pardon?

S: Somebody is always talking about the Czar!

H: Do you know the Czar?

S: Yes, yes, I know how he looks. He resembles my father.

H: I beg your pardon?

S: He resembles my father, but he is not my father!

H: Who is your father?

S: He is the Grand Duke.

H: The Grand Duke?

S: Yes.

H: And what about the Czar?

S: He wants to drive out the Grand Duke, but that is why my father can't, no . . .

H: What can't he?

S: I must keep quiet.

H: Aren't you allowed to talk about it?

S: No.

H: But you know about it?

S: Hm.

H: Can you tell me why you think you are bad or cruel? What are you doing to make you believe that?

S: I am avenging my father.

H: I beg your pardon?

S: Yes, I am avenging my father after—yes, because he is dead.

H: How did he die? How old were you when he died?

S: Nineteen.

H: And what caused your father's death?

S: Poison. I know exactly when he drank it.

H: Do you know who gave him the poison?

S: A marshall, someone we trusted. I never could stand him. He was in on the plot.

H: And?

S: The goblet—he drank out of it that evening. That was the one that had the rosettes. The goblet was smooth—it was the smooth one, and on the stem there were rosettes—and when I ran my finger across it and felt the rosettes . . . no, that isn't true, I can't say that . . .

H: What is not true?

S: I'm not allowed to say all that!

H: Why not? You can tell me. It won't make any difference. Tell me. What about the goblet?

S: I saw how he touched the goblet with his fingers, and I thought he was looking to see whether it was clean. That's when he must have put the poison into it or else . . . the rim of the goblet, he ran his fingers around it, and that's how the poison got into it. The rim of the goblet, and I had the feeling . . . I thought he was playing music. We used to do that often—make music with our fingers by rubbing them across the glasses, but then I wondered, this was the golden one. This could not produce music—and he ran his fingers across it. I should not have gone in, and that's why I did not tell anyone, because I always run off; I am always where I am not supposed to be.

H: Why were you not supposed to be there?

S: Well, I am only supposed to stay in the left wing.

H: Why?

S: Because I am only allowed in the left wing.

H: How old are you?

S: I am grown up. I'm nineteen.

H: Nineteen?

S: My father told me it is not nice for me to go out. It is indecent—and that's how I saw it.

H: Very well, let us continue. What happens next?

S: My mother is sick.

H: What is wrong with her?

S: She is lying in her bedroom and she is complaining of pains.

H: Has she been there long?

S: The people are saying "Nandi."

H: What does that mean?

S: They say mother is—she is going to die of grief.

H: Why?

S: Of grief—I don't know what the word means.

H: What is happening to your father?

S: They are carrying him into a vault . . . no, it is not a vault. People are going in and he is not being lowered. They are carrying the coffin in and simply placing it on the ground—a grave that you can look into. That can't be my father!

H: What is wrong with your father?

S: They have him in this open grave.

H: The coffin?

S: Yes, the people are walking past, carrying torches.

H: I beg your pardon?

S: The flames are burning—they are torches—father always liked torches, and mother wanted the candlestick. He always said he wanted . . . he loved torchlight. When the people came to the castle with their torches, he liked those lights—then he always put his arm around my shoulder.

H: I beg your pardon?

S: He always put his arm around my shoulder and said that he liked this light. It was natural light.

H: What? The torches?

S: Yes, that's why there are torches beside his grave.

H: Is the grave far from your house?

S: Hm, I don't know what is far. If I run far, if I leave the castle and run for a long time, I can run for days—that's far. I don't know—I don't understand time. I think that for me there is no time.

H: Do you know what year your father died?

S: 1800 . . . no [*cries*].

H: What is so bad about that? Tell me!

S: Mother had the date removed from the gravestone.

H: The date?

S: Yes.

H: Why?

S: Because she said the earth should have stood still, and because it didn't do that, it is a damned year.

H: What was the year on the gravestone?

S: I don't know anymore. Maybe seventy—I don't know, I really don't know.

H: You are nineteen years old?

S: Yes.

H: In what city and in what locality did this happen? Where are you living? Can you tell me that?

S: Two days from Petersburg.

H: And does your city have a name?

S: Oh, yes.

H: Yes?

S: I am dizzy.

H: You don't have to tell me. Can you tell me your father's name?

S: Nicolai.

H: I beg your pardon?

S: Nicolai, Duke of . . . [*greatly agitated*].

H: Please, what were you about to say? You don't feel well?

S: They are always crying for bread.

H: The people are crying for bread?

S: They are crying for . . .

H: What people are these?

S: They are all standing in front of the window.

H: In front of the window?

S: Yes, far down below—they are raising up their arms and crying for "chleb." *

H: Tell me more.

S: I cannot walk. I am standing still and can no longer feel my legs because I am so touched by that—and my mother only smiles because we have plenty to eat. I cannot stand that. I think I am going to faint.

H: What happens next?

S: I no longer have any feeling in my legs.

H: What else is happening?

S: Someone is coming and they are carrying me away. I have no more feeling in my legs—from up here [*points to her thighs*].

H: What happens now?

---

* Russian = bread.

S: I find it so unjust that we have everything and the others cannot live. And they have children, too. I hate my mother.

H: What is her name?

S: Catherine—I hate her—I hate her. I will never forget how they were standing there and shouting.

H: Tell me all about it. Come, tell me.

S: This . . .

H: Who? What?

S: This man, he is a healer.

H: What is that?

S: They always call him when mother has pains. He puts things on your skin.

H: What does he put on your skin?

S: All sorts of animals.

H: What do they look like?

S: Leeches, I think.

H: Leeches?

S: Yes.

H: Is that so unpleasant?

S: It looks terrible—and everyone says that I am pale.

H: How old are you now?

S: I am ten, no twelve—I was just twelve. I'm never sure of my age because I'm too small—and they always say I am ten, but I am twelve.

H: Do you know what year this is?

S: We don't write the years. The teacher forbids it.

H: Why?

S: Because the years are counted.

H: What does she say?

S: The years are counted.

H: And that is why you don't write them?

S: Yes.

H: But you know what year this is, don't you?

S: Yes, but I don't want to say it. I won't say it.

H: Will you tell me in what year you were born?

S: 1851.

H: Yes.

S: But I'm not allowed to say it . . .

H: What else would you like to tell me?

S: I want to get rid of those pictures.

H: What pictures.

S: Pictures of those hungry people down there, pictures of those people who crowd around us and follow us.

H: Are you afraid of them?

S: I'm afraid of them, and my father is afraid that they will do something to me—because they know I'm his favorite.

H: Do you have brothers and sisters?

S: Yes.

H: How many?

S: Two.

H: Sisters?

S: Yes, and then there is one son, but he does not belong to our family.

H: But he is a son?

S: Yes.

H: Of your father?

S: Yes.

H: But why doesn't he belong to your family?

S: Because my mother doesn't like him.

H: Does he live with you?

S: Yes, he is with us a great deal.

H: Good. Let us go along a little further in your life. You are getting older. You are getting to be fifteen years old. How are you? You are fifteen years old.

S: I am always in the halls. I'd rather be there than in the throne room or in the park. It's always the same thing. I don't like that at all. I don't like it. I'd rather read.

H: What are you reading now?

S: A very fat book, but my father forbid me to read it.

H: What is the name of it?

S: It's about a battle, about a battle, and it's no book for me. It's very hard for me to read because the letters are so crooked.

H: But you are reading it anyway?

S: I have to hide it.

H: Is it exciting? Do you like it?

S: There are heroes.

H: Yes.

S: And they act as if only heroes can lead a happy life. I find that untrue, but I will read further.

H: Good. You are getting older. You are getting to be seventeen, nineteen. Tell me something.

S: [*Sobs*]

H: What is the matter?

S: People are evil.

H: Why?

S: There are so many hypocrites. My father said that there were many hypocrites around me. They pretend to be friends. My father is not feeling well.

H: Why not?

S: He has worries.

H: Why?

S: He does not meet with the council as often as he used to.

H: With whom?

S: With the men, with the councillors.

H: Who are they? Do you know any of them?

S: There are many of them. They meet in a room and talk. One talks in behalf of the people, another for the affairs of the crown, another for . . .

H: And what else?

S: For the dukes, no, for the barons, the estates, for the affairs of the estates.

H: And what is your father?

S: My father is a Grand Duke.

H: And he meets with these people frequently?

S: Yes, whenever he comes out, I have to act like a little child and dance around like a little girl in order to cheer him up. I want to help him as much as possible with this, with his difficult problems, and he always wants to keep me a little girl and not bother me with his troubles.

H: What happens now?

S: I keep worrying him because I don't do what I am supposed to.

H: For example?

S: I run away and I am gone for days.

H: Where do you go?

S: I go through the park where there is a little gate and then I disappear. There are fields and I have a dress that I borrow from a girl who cuts flowers back there—and I blackmail her and wear her dress over mine.

H: What is this blackmail?

S: I blackmail her. I once saw her making love to somebody, and I told her I am going to tell, I am going to tell. There is an overseer, and I told her that I would tell him if she did not do what I wanted her to do. So I always ask her for her dress, she lets me have it, and I run off. Then I'm gone for two days.

H: Where do you sleep?

S: I come back and then I hear that my father circulates stories about me to the effect that I am sick, that I am not well, because he knows that I want to be outside because otherwise I would choke.

H: Where do you sleep when you run away? What do you exist on? What do you eat?

S: I always visit a family that used to work for us. My father gave them a farm because he likes them. They are very old people, and they once served my father well. I always go there and I hear from them that the unrest is increasing.

H: What happens next?

S: It is unbelievably beautiful country. It is a plain, a large plain where you cannot even see the other end. There are fields and more fields. I love this world, but we will have to return to Petersburg.

H: Who are we?

S: All of us.

H: What do you mean by return to Petersburg? What do you do there?

S: We live there.

H: Do you have a house there?

S: We have one there and we live there. Six months of the year we are there in Petersburg.

H: What do you mean by there? Is it far away?

S: It is two days away. We always start in the evening and drive through the whole night and the entire day.

H: So you are going back to Petersburg?

S: I don't want to go to Petersburg!

H: Why don't you want to go there?

S: I don't like Petersburg. It's so cold and there is always so much snow. Once when I was looking out the window, out of the watchtower window . . .

H: What are you saying?

S: Petersburg with all its music—we are—we leave it often because everything is such a lie there. It only seems . . . We are only allowed to travel on certain streets. Hm—

H: What is the matter?

S: I have . . . [*becomes agitated*].

H: What is wrong?

S: I always have to fight it because . . . I always want to leave—I want to go away—to see what is in back of those streets on which we are not allowed to travel. There must be more.

H: More of what?

S: The beggars are always chased away. One of them once buried himself in the snow so that they could not chase him, and I saw him standing there—dead—and since then I cannot rest because I know they are shielding us from them, from the needs of others.

H: Whom do you mean?

S: Myself.

H: And whom else?

S: My father. They tell him there is contentment, that the people are content, that the farmers have enough to eat, but that is all untrue. They are telling lies, these councillors, they are just humoring him. I told Papa about this dead man who was standing there and he closed my eyes. He put his hands over my eyes and said, "There are things that one must not see. We are only human; we cannot provide justice for everyone." My father speaks of things that you can read in books.

H: What do you mean by that?

S: My father is a wise and good man.

H: How old are you?

S: Twenty-one.

H: What does your father do?

S: There is no father anymore.

H: Since when? Tell me about it. Tell me the whole story.

S: My father is dead. Hm, hm.

H: How long?

S: Sixteen months.

H: Tell me how it happened.

S: My father was poisoned. We are now in Petersburg and everything is terrible. I would like to die in the snow.

H: Why?

S: [*Cries*]

H: Come, tell me, why do you want to die in the snow? Why? Tell me. Don't stop talking.

S: I don't want to live anymore.

H: Why don't you want to live anymore?

S: I don't like people anymore.

H: Because they poisoned your father?

S: Yes, and because my mother is so cruel.

H: And now you want to die?

S: Yes.

H: And what are you doing or what will you do?

S: I'm going to bury myself in the snow and die with nature, outside.

H: Are you really doing that? How old are you?

S: I am twenty-one.

H: Are you carrying out your plan?

S: No, no. [*breathes heavily*]

H: Well, tell me what is happening. What are you thinking about? What are you doing?

S: I'm in bed; I'm not feeling well.

H: What is wrong?

S: I have pneumonia.

H: You did go out into the snow?

S: Yes.

H: And now you are lying in bed?

S: Hm.

H: How old are you now? Twenty-one?

S: Yes.

H: Tell me. What happens now? Will you get well again?

S: Yes.

H: Let us go forward in time. How old will you get to be in this life? Can you tell me?

S: Sixty-one.

H: We will go further and further back in time. The picture will fade away . . .

Second Session

H: We are going back in time, back to the time of conception. We will go past conception, back further in time. We will go back in time until you find yourself in a new situation. There you will stop and describe what you observe. You will go back until you find yourself in a new situation. When you get there, tell me what is going on and what you see. Who is there?

S: I see an old woman.

H: Yes.

S: She is thin and bony.

H: Tell me something about her.

S: An old woman.

H: What is she doing?

S: She is sitting in, she is sitting on, on an armchair—no, it is not an armchair. What is it?

H: What is it? Describe it!

S: It has armrests and it is high. It is not a throne, but it is a —I don't want to . . .

H: What don't you want?

S: It must not be a throne. I don't want it to be a throne!

H: Just tell me what you see. So it is an armchair like a throne?

S: Yes.

H: And a woman is sitting on it?

S: Yes.

H: And what is she doing?

S: She has a black lace kerchief over her head, she has white hair and looks very cold.

H: Yes.

S: And she taps with her fingers, with her bony fingers, and constantly keeps tapping on the armrest.

H: Is she saying anything?

S: She is angry.

H: What is she saying?

S: I'm afraid that this is I. She is angry, no. How do I see the picture? She is angry, but why?

H: Just describe what you see.

S: [*Moans*]

H: Tell me more about what you see.

S: [*Moans again*]

H: What is happening?

S: The chair is on a platform, and there are high, very high, windows with satin drapes, very high windows with satin drapes that have a pattern.

H: Are there other people in the room?

S: Yes, many men who are standing there very humbly—I don't want, I don't want . . .

H: Let us leave this impression and go back about five years. We shall go back five years, and you will describe what you are doing. What are you doing?

S: I am in the park.

H: And what are you doing there?

S: I am walking through flowers. They have been planted. The flowers have been planted in beds. There is an unending large and wide meadow, a green carpet. I am in the back part of the park. Everything is peaceful, but I will destroy it.

H: You will destroy it?

S: Yes, I will destroy it all.

H: How old are you now?

S: Sixty.

H: And how will you destroy it? What will you do?

S: [*Moans*]

H: What are you planning to do?

S: I will be as cruel as always.

H: What do you mean by always?

S: Just as I was all my life. I don't like this peace. Everything radiates peace. I can't stand it.

H: What is wrong?

S: I would have to tell you so much.

H: Then tell me.

S: It is too much!

H: Start anywhere.

S: It is endless. I cannot justify why I am the way I am.

H: You do not need to justify yourself. Just tell us. I need no justification, just keep talking.

S: Even the twittering birds bother me. I see hypocrites everywhere: Everyone looks false to me. I'm happy that I can destroy it all.

H: Why? Does it make you happy to destroy everything?

—*199*

S: No, but I have the feeling that I can unhook something.

H: How will you destroy this? How will you do it? Give me an example.

S: I will buy people, people who can throw suspicion on persons whom I do not like, and then I will punish them, even though I know it is all lies and instigated by me. I will destroy everything.

H: How long have you been doing this? Since when did you feel this need to be cruel? Is it connected with your father?

S: Yes.

H: When did it start? When did you first notice this?

S: When I was nineteen. When my father died.

H: But your mother was still living then?

S: Yes.

H: Did you like your mother?

S: No, I liked my father. I always loved him.

H: What happened after your father's death? What happened to you? What did you do then?

S: My mother was deceitful, but that was so long ago, I don't want to talk about it. She was always deceitful. I always judged her correctly. I only lived to avenge my father. I lived my whole life that way.

H: How did you plan to avenge your father?

S: I wanted to destroy all those people who claimed to be friends. I am telling you this because it is so long ago.

H: You can tell me. Keep talking and tell me more.

S: Even the birds are driving me crazy here, these creatures that sing and act as if everything in life were beautiful. They deceive people. They ought to be shot. Something ought to be done with them. I will decree that there are to be no more birds in this country. There is to be not one single bird in my entire principality.

H: What sort of principality is this of which you speak?

S: I will decree it. It will be a decree!

H: What principality are you talking about?

S: It is my realm. I will order it done.

H: What realm are you speaking of?

S: The realm of my father.

H: What is the name of the realm? Does it have a name?

S: Of course!

H: What is it called?

S: Why do you ask me that?

H: Why don't you tell me?

S: You must know the borders of our realm.

H: I would like to hear the name. Tell me the name. Why won't you say it?

S: I would like to know why you want to know this.

H: Because I am a stranger and don't know it!

S: What are you doing here? What are you looking for and why are you here if you are a stranger? What did you lose?

H: Please don't be angry with me. There's no reason for it. Tell me more about your life.

S: Who are you? Who are you?

H: I am a voice speaking with you. You can tell me everything, even what you would not tell any other human being. I am no danger for you. I am here to help you.

S: No one helps me. No one helps me.

H: Speak to me. Tell me something of your life. What was the most beautiful event of your life?

S: My child, my child . . .

H: Did you give birth to a child?

S: No, not I. It is my child, but it does not belong to me.

H: To whom does it belong?

S: It does not belong to me. I did not give birth to it. It is a relative of mine. It is a little boy.

H: What is his name?

S: Alexei.

H: What is it?

S: That was the most beautiful event in my life.

H: What sort of event was it? Was it when the child came to you or when it was born? What did this event consist of?

S: The child was taken from me. He went back to his mother.

H: How long did he stay with you?

S: One spring, just one spring.

H: Do you have a husband?

S: I had many husbands. I married many men, but they would not touch me. They are all afraid of me.

H: Are you proud of your cruelty?

S: No, I do this because I am forced to. I cannot experience happiness because I know the end of happiness. Everything has an end and I have seen it. For this reason, I do this. That is why I use force. I also begrudge people the joy of doing something that would be good for them. I know I am evil.

H: Is there anything specific in your life that you regret?

S: I would have to regret my whole life. I am old.

H: How old?

S: Sixty.

H: What year is this?

S: Why do you want to know that?

H: I want to know what year it is.

S: Why do you want to know that? You are a voice. What do you want with me?

H: I ask questions. I do not answer questions. What year is this?

S: Nineteen hundred and something, but you must know that.

H: What is "and something"?

S: Eleven, twelve.

H: 1911?

S: Yes, I think so.

H: What is the name of the country that you rule over?

S: It bothers me. It bothers me, your questioning. I am wondering how you got here.

H: It is good for you to answer questions. It will help you look over your life.

S: My heart is beginning to pound again. Leave me alone.

H: Do you have trouble with your heart?

S: No one is ever there when you need help. I need this liquid that I hold under my nose, but no one is ever there. I ought to treat these people even more harshly than I do.

H: I will perform a service for you. I will get you this liquid. The scent will do you good. You need only breathe in and you will smell the scent which you need. Smell it and notice how good it is for you.

S: [*Takes a deep breath*]

H: Do you notice it?

S: No, I only smell air [*takes another breath*].

H: No, that can't be right!

S: [*Takes another deep breath*]

H: You will smell the scent of your smelling bottle.

S: [*Takes another breath*]

H: Your heart has stopped pounding and you are feeling better, right?

S: It is a different scent, but it does me good. At the moment I smell nothing, but I feel better.

H: I am here at your service whenever you need me.

S: I am not going to turn everything I have learned upside down because of you.

H: What have you learned? Tell me.

S: I have—I am tired.

H: What have you learned?

S: Why should I talk to you? I never had anyone all my life.

H: That is why I have come to you. Do you want to choke on your problems?

S: I will survive. I won't choke on them. I am too strong and powerful.

H: Is that what you have learned?

S: No, that is not it. That is a result of it. I believe I have grown up with every possible crime. I am, I had to fight myself because, after all, I am vulnerable, and each time it was a step forward. Now I am getting dizzy . . .

H: Why? Why are you getting dizzy? Because of what you have done or because of your power?

S: I see someone behind me who is watching me. When I am in that part of the park, no one else has any business there unless I call them. He is watching me. He has no business there. I'll have him beaten! [*breathes heavily*]

H: In your opinion, what was the cruelest thing you ever did?

S: I had the councillors beheaded.

H: Who were they?

S: Those who were around me, but that was a long time ago.

H: When was that? How old were you then?

S: I was still young. It was when my mother—no, I don't want to talk about it.

H: Why not? Are you sorry now?

S: No, no, then I would have to be sorry about my whole life. I regret nothing. No, no, I knew what I was doing. They can't tell me I had a guilty conscience. I will have to bear that alone.

H: That is correct. I won't tell you that, either. I simply asked because you said you did not want to talk about it.

S: It was a long time ago. It was a lifetime ago, and I am old. Nothing bothers me anymore.

H: When you were very young and your father was still alive, you felt sorry for the beggars and you disliked injustice. Do you ever think back on that time?

S: I suffered a great deal.

H: How?

S: I was at everyone's disposal. Anyone could wound me. I was there to intercede for all. I was impartial, I was human and I lived a life that does not exist, because I had only happiness. All that has died. I choked it when I no longer wanted to live after my father died. One must never get as attached to one person as I did, otherwise one cannot go on living.

H: Is that also one of the things you have learned?

S: That was what influenced my life. I should have lived it differently. I could not have gone on like that. I never trusted anyone again, never. And I never will again. Now I am asking myself why I tell you all this, and I am not going to tell you anything more. If you are a voice, go away and leave me alone. Don't follow me.

H: Oh, I won't do that. But is there anyone on the outside of whom you might be afraid?

S: No, I have built too many walls around me. My cruelty has been well circulated and no one will dare do anything to me. They are afraid of me—and the Czar is favorably disposed toward me.

H: What is the name of the Czar?

S: You ask me dates, yes, you ask me dates, and now you ask me names.

H: Yes, and you will tell me.

S: I will have you expelled!

H: Oh, yes, you can do that, but first you must tell me the name of the Czar.

S: Aren't you from this area?

H: What is the name of the Czar?

S: You aren't from here?

H: No.

S: You are avoiding that. What do you want? You waited until I was here alone.

H: I can do that anywhere.

S: You ask me for the name of my country—you ask about him . . .

H: Are you afraid?

S: I am old. What do you want with me?

H: I asked whether you are afraid. Are you?

S: No.

H: Well, then . . .

S: I don't want to. That is not fear. I will not listen to you.

H: No.

S: I don't know. I can't handle you.

H: Does that make you angry?

S: You make me restless. I am old. Leave me alone.

H: Oh, don't worry. I will leave you, if you like. I am only having a conversation with you. Not everyone who talks with you wants to make changes. I don't want to make any changes.

S: But you want to know everything!

H: Yes.

S: I should not have talked to you. I am going to close my ears. Besides, I am going away now. I am leaving.

H: Hm, where to?

S: Women will come to me who will want to make changes. I will listen to them, but I am not going to listen to you anymore. People have always done what I wanted and I don't trust you.

H: I noticed that, but you are completely wrong.

S: I want nothing more to do with you.

H: That doesn't matter. I am going to take the liberty of visiting you once more, and this time it will be in a new situation.

S: What good will it do you? What good will it do me? It does nothing for me. [*She speaks softly to herself.*] Besides, the sun is going down, and I am going in—I am going in. I said that they could come when the sun goes down. I like this twilight. It gives me a pleasant feeling. It gives me the feeling that I am still alive. It is the twilight that I like. I will live once more. Everyone expects something of me, and I will have to disappoint them. I intend to disappoint them. The sentiment is good, however. I will have an ear for the women. Perhaps I will do something worthwhile for them, which I have rarely done. This voice has made me restless, but it's not going to bother me. So many people have gone through my hands, why should something disembodied do something to me? What did that voice ask me? It wants information. It probably wants to accuse me of something or perhaps accuse him of something. I was asking for his name, always asking for his name. Something is wrong there. I will have to call the wise men together. I can't get any further. There was this one man who spoke very intelligently; I have heard that he is a philosopher. I will ask him what sort of intentions could be behind that voice. It is very pleasant here. It is cool and pleasant.

H: Let us leave this impression and go forward a year. You are a year older. What are you doing?

S: I am lying in bed.

H: Yes, and how do you feel?

S: Not well.

H: What is wrong?

S: I don't know. Just old age, I guess. I think that the people who are around me are under the impression that I am no longer here. I am talking to myself. I trust no one anymore and I withdraw myself and stay in bed. Then I can see what's going on. My windows, I've had the curtains removed so that no one can hide behind them. The windows are bare and it is cold, but I can look out. I'm staying in bed, in a large bed, but I don't feel well.

H: What is wrong with you?

S: Who are you? Who are you?

H: What is your name?

S: Who are you?

H: Forget your mistrust. It is easier if you will simply tell me your name.

S: Who are you that you can come into my bedroom and ask me my name? Who are you?

H: There is no need to get yourself excited. Just stay calm.

S: No, I am old and I am weak.

H: Let us try a little experiment. You don't want to tell me your name. Well, I am going to count to three and when I say "three," you will find yourself saying your name without any difficulty. One, two, three!

S: [*Moans*]

H: Tell me your name. Your mouth will say it all by itself!

S: [*Moans and whispers inaudibly*]

H: Now you've said it, but say it once more out loud!

S: [*Moans and grimaces with her mouth*]

H: Say it out loud!

S: [*Moans*]

H: Do you know your name?

S: My heart pains me! [*displays a pain-distorted expression*]

H: Your pain is leaving you, and you will feel well again, very well. You will suddenly find your pain disappearing. I will count to three and the pain will be gone. One, two, three. You will breathe quietly and evenly and you will feel very, very well. You feel very well now, right?

S:[*Breathes heavily*]

H: Do you notice that you are beginning to feel better?

S: [*Continues breathing*]

H: Do you notice that you are feeling better? Oh, you are feeling much, much better. Admit it!

S: I feel dizzy.

H: No, you are feeling very well, isn't that right? Aren't you feeling better?

S: [*Breathes more easily*]

H: Very well, now I will leave you alone.

S: [*Breathes freely*]

H: Let us leave this impression and go forward in time. The pictures will fade into the background, and we shall go forward, constantly forward. You are quiet and peaceful and calm and will continue to go forward in time. We shall go forward until we reach the year 1975. That is how far we shall go. We will not look at any details as time passes. We will simply go forward until we get to 1975. You are sleeping soundly. You are quiet, very quiet. You are feeling well. You are sleeping deeply and soundly. Your whole body is relaxed. You are feeling well. The pictures are fading into the background. The pictures have disappeared, and now you hear only my voice. You are breathing quietly and evenly. You are feeling well, happy and content . . .

Birth
and
Death
in
Experiment

O UR REGRESSION EXPERIMENTS have given us the opportunity to hear exact and authentic descriptions of conception, embryo development, birth, death, and the post-mortal state. We experience not only the event itself, but obtain insight into the reliving of these developments. Many may doubt the authenticity of these reports, but it has frequently been possible to verify descriptions and statements about birth and the embryo condition with the aid of a subject's parents. Up to now, it has been possible to verify such statements in every instance. Details of the birth procedure, exact descriptions of the delivery room, the number of persons present, words that were spoken, abortion attempts, falls or fright situations of the mother during pregnancy—all these things can be verified in most cases where the parents of the subjects are still living.

After the reliability of statements with regard to birth and embryonic development has been established, it ought to be possible to attribute a high degree of authenticity to other statements that are more difficult to prove but that had the same, or similar, origins. In addition to this, we have the agreement of all subjects on their descriptions of death and the after-death condition. If one were to allow ten different individuals to describe an unknown situation such as the post-mortal state according to their respective imaginations, one would obtain ten different versions. During the regressions, however, there was not one single instance where a subject described anything that varied substantially from statements made by any of the others.

For these reasons, I should like to be permitted to offer a few thoughts on the consequences that must necessarily ensue on the basis of the experimental data obtained.

It is important for parents to know that their child possesses complete consciousness from the moment of conception, that he perceives all impressions and develops them. Consciousness is already present before a body even exists as such. At the time of conception, the first trauma is established if the parents are not in harmony, if one is intoxicated or if the mother attempts to put off her husband. The same thing happens as the result of conversations after sexual intercourse if the parents express their fear of having a child or their wish for a specific sex.

Once conception has taken place, the corporal life of the future child begins. From the first day, it experiences everything the mother experiences. It experiences the shock or joy of the mother when she becomes aware that she is pregnant. It experiences every sex act from its point of view. Many sexual problems and aversions find their source here. Although there is the danger that the parents, due to ignorance, may commit some serious blunders, there is also the opportunity to begin the child's education at this time. Prenatal education has been known for a long time, but has never been widely accepted. During pregnancy, it is very important that the mother begin to speak to the fully conscious child in her womb; during this period, she ought to occupy herself exclusively with pleasant things, listen to good music, read good literature, and so on. She should avoid all excitement and ugly impressions. I am sure it is unnecessary to point out what effect arguments between parents must have on a child.

If during this time the parents have done a good job "educating" their child, they may expect an effortless birth, free of complications. Birth is the moment during which nowadays everything that can be done wrong is automatically done wrong. Starting with artificially induced labor, which must of necessity contradict the natural rhythm of the cosmos, and finishing with an unconscious mother, the poor child experiences one shock after another. No wonder it cries out at birth. To call this crying a sign of well-being is the height of irony. When a child is brought into the world properly, it does not cry; it smiles. It ought to be made obligatory for all mothers-to-be to be made conscious of their own birth so that they can understand this event from the point of view of the child.

For nine months, the child is gently rocked in a dark, evenly heated cavern, when suddenly it experiences a "wonderful" poison entering its body through the umbilical cord. Birth can now begin. Once on the outside, large strange hands reach out for it, hold it up, give it a whack and cut the umbilical cord. It is bright and cold, and the child must now go it alone—from one minute to the next. It is put aside, can hardly see its mother, who is probably in an anesthetic sleep—the father is nowhere to be found—and to make up for that, a kind but strange nurse carries it away somewhere.

If all children come into the world this way, it is no wonder that today we have so many neurotics: "As ye sow, so shall ye reap." But there is one doctor who understands what happens at birth and what can be accomplished there. This is the French gynecologist Dr. Leboyer of Paris, the father of gentle birth. He has developed a birth technique in which all these trauma for the child (as well as the mother) are avoided. The mother brings her child into the world quietly in a darkened individual room. As soon as the child is born, it is placed on the mother's stomach, and the mother places her hands on the child. Mother and child remain connected by the umbilical cord. The father is present, of course. Everything happens slowly and naturally—all violent sensations are avoided. The child has only changed its position from inside to outside—no other changes have taken place. After a while, the umbilical cord is stroked gently toward the mother until the pulse becomes slower; the moment it stops, the cord is cut. Without a slap on the rear end, the child's own rhythm begins to awaken slowly and independently.

Although gentle birth in accordance with Dr. Leboyer's technique is the ideal method of bringing a child into the world correctly and naturally, medical circles are reluctant to adopt this practice. For this reason, it is up to the parents to decide how their child is to be brought into the world. Even if at first it is not possible for most people to provide the "gentle birth" for their child, at least a few points should be observed:

The father must be present at birth without fail. A child should never have to be born under anesthesia. Any and all injections should be kept to an absolute minimum. Induced labor should be avoided if at all possible. If this is unavoidable, acupuncture, homeopathy, or even infusion may be introduced, but never should drugs or manual pressure be used. One should insist that the child be placed in his mother's arms immediately after birth.

In connection with pregnancy, we always have the problem of abortion. The problem is actually very simple. The mother who aborts her child in its third month is doing the same thing as if she were killing her five-year-old child. There is no difference between murder in a mother's womb or murder outside of a mother's womb. Similarly, the size of the body of a human being should not justify a difference in judgment, otherwise in the future the punishment for murder would have to be correlated to the weight of the victim's body. And I am not concerned with whether abortion is "bad" or not. I am more concerned with the importance of logical thinking. If we are agreed that abortion is permissible, we should not complain when children or adults are murdered. But we live in a perverted world and find it normal. Seventy-five-year-old people are artificially kept alive in the intensive care unit of a clinic or, more aptly stated, are brutally prevented from dying, while embryos, on the other hand, are prevented from living.

Do not misunderstand me: I am not in favor of severe punishment for women and doctors who perform an abortion. Everyone must consider himself responsible for what he does. He who ends a physical life places himself opposite the law. He prepares the contents and must sooner or later redeem the form. It is not up to others to worry about atonement. This also pertains to all other crimes, including murder. If the law prohibits abortion, this is at best an effort to protect man from his own stupidity.

Nature has given man the choice of acting rightly or wrongly, within or without the law, and we ought to respect this freedom of choice. One should not, however, twist the clear facts of a case so that new ethics are born out of the subject of abortion. I have heard, for example, that in some countries doctors are forced by law to interrupt pregnancy. So long as we see the world as it is and then make conscious decisions, we cannot blame anyone else. Fortunately, life is indestructible. Man alone has the power to change matter—and cannot even do this right!

Birth and death are two aspects of one and the same thing. Once a person is born, death is the only thing that will be certain in his life. Every birth is at the same time a death, every death at the same time a birth. In both cases, we leave one existence in order to transfer to another. Almost all people have a great fear of dying, but they all have just as much fear of being born. This might, for example, sound like this:

S: I am in a large cavern.
H: Do you feel well?
S: Yes, it is warm and damp.
H: Will you stay here forever?
S: No.
H: What will happen to you?

S: I will have to get out.

H: Where to?

S: I must—I must get back on earth.

H: Are you looking forward to this?

S: No.

H: You are just being born. What is happening?

S: I am being pressed and squeezed—it is a feeling—I will have to leave here.

H: Do you like the feeling?

S: No.

H: Are you afraid?

S: Yes.

H: Of what?

S: This cozy feeling—I must get out of here—something is poking me—I am being pressed more and more—I suddenly see light—it is getting colder and colder and colder—I am coming into a room—a large, cold room—it is getting light—lighter and colder—I am being born.

H: You are in the world. Do you know what will happen next?

S: Yes, I must live.

H: Does this make you happy?

S: No, but it must be done!

For comparison purposes, here is the description of a birth by another subject:

S: I don't want to go out—I must leave, but I don't want to.

H: Why not?

S: It's not good on the outside.

H: Describe your experiences—how is it now?

S: Fine—it is so quiet and protected.

H: What do you see?

S: I see—no, I feel the warmth—the peace.

H: What do you taste?

S: I taste—it is somewhat sweet in my mouth——I don't know what it's called.

H: Proceed from the beginning to the end of your birth and describe what happens—you are just being born.

S: This is it—I wanted to stay inside, but I must leave now. It's most unusual—yes, it's getting lighter now—it's brighter out —something is pulling on me—I don't want to—I don't want to!

H: What do you feel?

S: Oh, everything is so—they're grabbing me—this is—now I'm out of—out of the protective—it's all so—different.

H: What is it like? Describe your experience!

S: They're holding me. I feel big hands—something—is seizing me—it is—light—but I don't see anything—I just feel.

H: Why can't you see?

S: I don't know—everything looks so blurred—then—

H: Well, look around. What does the room look like?

S: I don't recognize anything—everything is so bright—so far—

H: What is happening now?

S: They are picking me up again—and putting me down—in a—I don't know what it's called—a crib—now they're lifting me up again.

H: Was there anything in your birth that bothered you?

S: I—I would rather not have left the cavern.

H: Is there anything else that was done wrong?

S: No.

H: Let us go back in time again. We shall go back to the time before your birth—the period during which you were in this cavern. In this period between conception and birth, pick out a decisive event—any event that caused any kind of feeling.

S: I know I have to be born—yes, I see my life before me— but I don't want to return to the world. Why must I come back? What did I do?

H: Why will you have to return?

S: I don't know—there was a point—now I'm afraid of—of life.

H: Why?

S: Because it will be very difficult.

The examples can be continued ad infinitum. Birth is the end of life for the embryo. It is only natural that the embryo is deathly afraid. But just as birth is not the actual end of life, death is not the end of human life. While he is very much afraid of this step, man, as soon as he has died, feels remarkably well in his new state.

Having died means the point in time at which the astral body completely separated from the physical body. Consciousness, the id-identity, and all sensual perception are in the astral body. This is the body of the psyche. Since all sensual perception is found in the astral body, man can see and hear just as well after leaving the body as before. It is one of the ingrained errors of our time to consider sensual perception a product of our physical senses. The physical organs of our body are only the material equivalent of psychic sensual perception.

One need not die to obtain this experience. It is possible to learn the technique of astral wandering by the use of certain exercises. Among these is the conscious departure from the material body. The ego awareness is always completely in the astral body; through these departures, one can see one's own physical body from the outside. Many people have had this experience spontaneously without training—and usually such a surprising departure from the body creates great fear. Anyone who cannot imagine the process of astral wandering and therefore does not believe in it must make the effort to learn this conscious departure by himself. After that, he will know from his own experience that man does not see with the physical eye, does not hear with his ears, and does not think with his brain.

The astral body steps out in every case of unconsciousness. For this reason, a person can see and hear everything while his body is unconscious. Under hypnosis, it is possible to make known the entire procedure of an operation. If everyone knew what the anesthetized person can perceive, doctors would be much more careful about their comments and conversations during and immediately after an operation. Every word spoken during this condition drifts unhindered, as in deep hypnosis, as a suggestion into the subconscious of the "unconscious" person. Little remarks such as "that looks horrible" or "that will take a long time to heal" may make a difference in the future health of the patient. By the same token, a well-aimed, positive suggestion might cut the postoperative recuperating time in half.

As an example of how a person can experience the condition of unconsciousness from the perspective of the astral body, we repeat here a segment of a reincarnation report. The event took place in 1850 near Lake Constance:

S: I had an accident.

H: Let us dissolve to the time of this accident. Tell us what is happening. Where are you and what is going on?

S: Yes, but my sisters must not learn of this. My sisters must know nothing of this.

H: What must they not learn? What—that you are going to have a baby?

S: No, they must not know that. Otherwise my father will know it, too.

H: Well, tell me; what is happening?

S: Well, I have a friend, and I think I am going to have his baby. One evening when we saw each other, I told him this. He said let's meet at the lake.

H: When, the same evening?

S: No, two days later?

H: What time of day?

S: Five o'clock in the afternoon.

H: What month is this?

S: September.

H: September what?

S: When we meet at the lake? September 18.

H: What year?

S: 1850.

H: You are meeting at the lake. You agreed to meet there?

S: Yes.

H: Tell us what is going on!

S: Well, I arrive at the lake, and he is already sitting there and I go to him. He must have heard me—he gets up, turns around, and looks at me. He has such a horrible expression on his face—I am terribly afraid—he intends to do something dreadful to me.

H: What happens?

S: He puts one arm around me and turns me around. I don't know what's going on, but he steps back. He has a heavy object in his hand. I can't see it clearly, but everything happens very quickly.

H: What is happening quickly? What is he doing?

S: He strikes out at me and hits me on the head. I get dizzy and fall into the water.

H: Into the water?

S: Yes.

H: Deep?

S: I don't know—I only know I am getting all wet.

H: What happens next? Tell me exactly. What happens now? You are in the water?

S: I saw another man just before I fell in—an older man. I am in the water now and see nothing. Suddenly my body rises to the top, and I see my friend standing there. He evidently has also noticed that someone else is nearby and drops something.

H: What does he drop?

S: Sort of a stick in the shape of a club, all full of blood. He drops it. The man comes running up, sees my body in the water, comes up to me, pulls me out. I don't look very pretty—my face is smeared with blood, my head is open, and blood is pouring out. He pulls me out, leaves me lying there, puts me down, and folds my hands together. He can run pretty fast, even though he seems to be fairly old.

H: Where is your friend? Did he run away, too?

S: Yes, but he is not running after him. He is running off in a different direction.

H: Well, what happens now?

S: I see my body lying there. It seems to be fading away.

H: The body?

S: Yes.

H: Just keep looking down. What happens next?

S: It is getting less and less clear. Suddenly I feel—someone comes running toward me—a man with a cart—an empty hay wagon—they put me on it—very carefully, on top of some pillows and blankets.

H: Is it only one man or are there others?

S: There are two men and they take me to a doctor.

H: Yes, and what does he do?

S: I don't know—I have such a headache.

H: Don't feel the headache, and tell me what else is happening. Just look—don't feel. I will remove your headache, and you will continue to tell me what you see.

S: Yes.

H: Do you feel it getting better?

S: Yes, yes—I don't know—he's bandaging me and says the most important thing is to stop the bleeding. The blood must stop flowing. He puts a large wrapping around my head and gives me tablets.

H: Are you conscious again or are you still unconscious?

S: I think I'm regaining consciousness.

H: Are you saying anything? Are you talking to the doctor?

S: No, I just keep saying, "It hurts, it hurts."

H: Can you hear what is being said? Is the man who found you saying anything to the doctor? Is he telling him what happened to you?

S: No, they are saying I will have to go to the hospital. But that—that will take a long time. They will have to get me there quickly.

H: How are they taking you there?

S: With a big carriage.

H: Is it a long trip?

S: Yes, it seems like a long trip. Now I'm entering the hospital—they're putting me in a bed and giving me more tablets—no, they're opening up the bandages, and now they have to sew me up.

This subject gave a beautiful description of what happened to her in a state of unconsciousness. We see that she was in mortal danger when she said, "I see my body lying there. It seems to be fading away. It is getting less and less clear." Had nothing else happened, she probably would have died. She would have been so far removed from her body that she could not have returned. Because of the man who put her body into the wagon, the astral body is "suddenly" attracted back to the physical body —and it is possible for life to continue.

There are a number of scientists who are collecting reports of people who had been considered clinically dead and were brought back to life. These reports are all the same. No one has yet said that death was anything unpleasant. The mere fact that anyone can make a statement about this proves the independence of consciousness, which can exist without a body. The one thing considered unpleasant is "being called back."

Our age and our culture have developed a fanaticism that requires that people be kept alive and be prevented from dying. What is the underlying reason for this unnatural and paradoxical attitude? This development has progressed to such an extent that the individual hardly finds it possible to protect himself against costly resuscitation experiments. Modern intensive care units are under pressure to accomplish something for the sake of prestige. The dying man becomes the victim of medical thoughts of success. Thus the ability to do something becomes a reason for doing. Action no longer depends on need but on thoughts of functional progress. Medicine no longer exists for man, but man for medicine. Old people in old folks' homes are forming groups of mutual interest and with the help of lawyers are trying to assure themselves of help from an intensive care unit in case of emergency.

The background for this development appears relatively easy

to explain, in my opinion. Because of his materialistic philosophy, man has been deprived of his natural understanding of death as a rhythmic change to a different level of existence and has been given the substitute claim that "when death comes, all is ended." This creates a frantic clinging to life and a panicky fear of nothingness. This rarely admitted fear of death projects itself from one person to the next. Every death and every threat of death becomes the screen on which we reflect our own fear. The death of another always reminds us of our own imminent death and brings closer the threat to our own life.

The person who has not come to terms with death will usually suppress the idea and live in the expectation that he will live forever. A death, however, will quickly release him from this illusion. Fear suddenly appears. By attempting to save someone else from death, he attempts to remove his own fears. He wants to prove to himself that something can be done against death—that one need not simply yield to it. The attempt to maintain life at any price is in reality the attempt to prevent one's illusion from collapsing. Thus lifesaving has become a sport; it is not by chance that we speak of "a race with death."

Such activity does not jibe with the concept of reincarnation. If we observe the cultures in which the idea of rebirth is firmly anchored, we find an entirely different attitude toward death. Europeans cannot understand how people are permitted to die in India. For the Hindu as well as the Buddhist, however, birth and death are nothing special. One is acquainted with the life cycle, one feels himself embedded in a higher order of things without attempting diligently to force nature to proceed in the direction that man considers best. This inner peace makes it possible at the moment of death to do the only thing that is necessary: to help the dying to die. After all, we help at birth and don't try to push the child back into the womb. Why should we do the reverse at death? Here, too, it would be fitting to help make it easier for the dying to be released from the material world and make possible his birth on the other side.

All my subjects repeatedly experience their deaths in every

detail during our sessions. Thereafter they have a new attitude toward life and death. They learn to organize their lives within a larger scope without fleeing from the present. Anyone who looks over his incarnations knows the importance of living within the law in the here and now. Miss M., a student, twenty years of age, who was also the subject of the last report, is at present reviewing her past four lives in every detail. In one of the last sessions, we tried to view this chain of incarnations as a whole. Here is a portion of that session:

H: Let us proceed in your life to the next important event.

S: I have a fairly high fever.

H: What is wrong?

S: I don't know.

H: Was it sudden?

S: Yes.

H: How old are you?

S: I feel so bad—I'm going to die.

H: How old are you? What year is this?

S: Thirty-eight—1668.

H: What is happening?

S: I am shivering—I'm hot—I will have to die, but I don't want to leave my husband alone. No—I don't want to leave him alone—he is kneeling next to me—everything is getting so weird.

H: What is getting weird?

S: The room—everything is turning black—no, no, I don't want to—I don't want to!

H: What is happening? Tell us!

S: I don't know—heavy pressure—very heavy pressure—then I'm surrounded—something is lifting me up—I see myself lying there.

H: What else do you see?

S: My husband.

H: What are you experiencing? What do you feel?

S: I'm so sorry that he is grieving—but it's no use. He'll have to get used to it.

H: How are you?

S: Fine.

H: Do you feel any pain or do you have any complaints?

S: No.

H: Where are you?

S: I am simply there.

H: And what do you see, since you say you see yourself?

S: Well, my body.

H: And where are you? No longer in your body?

S: No.

H: What is your feeling toward your body—and what sort of relationship do you have with it?

S: None whatsoever—I needed it—but not anymore.

H: Do you see anything in the immediate future? Something connected with this happening? Do you see a funeral or anything like that?

S: Yes, yes, they are burying me—in the garden—but it's very unclear.

H: How do you feel now?

S: Very well.

H: Do you wish for anything?

S: No.

H: What will happen now? You will stay here now, won't you?

S: No. I can't stay here.

H: Why not? Don't you like it here?

S: Yes, but I must return to the world once more. My fate has not yet been fulfilled.

H: Can it be fulfilled?

S: Yes.

H: So you will come back to earth once more?

S: Yes.

H: And will it be fulfilled then?

S: No.

H: Are you glad to be coming back to earth again?

S: No.

H: Why not?

S: Because it will be difficult for me. I will have to struggle. It won't be as good as it is here.

H: Were you satisfied with your last life? Looking at it from your present point of view, would you do anything differently? Do you believe you made an important mistake?

S: No, just many small mistakes.

H: From where you are now, what would you especially want to do if you were to live this life again?

S: I would try to think better of people and learn to like them as they are.

H: Will you do that in your next life?

S: No.

H: Let us move forward in time until you come back into the world again.

S: I feel a strong suction.

H: What is happening to you?

S: Some sort of power is pulling me down—always further and further—I can't explain it. A big canyon is pulling me down—then suddenly everything is gone. It's as if I were a ball that is being pressed by two hands. It gets smaller and smaller. Then all is suction and it pulls on me. Now it's all over.

H: Do you feel well now?

S: No, I know that I must live a life now.

H: So you will be born in a few months?

S: Yes.

H: You are being born. Tell me the year!

S: 1834.

H: You are back on earth. You are growing up. You are getting older, right?

S: Yes.

H: What is your name?

S: Anna.

H: How old are you now?

S: Fifteen.

H: Let us go further. You are twenty, thirty, forty.

S: Yes.

H: Let us go further forward until this life is ended, too. What is happening?

S: I have such a terrible headache. I will probably have to die.

H: Go through this event and describe what is happening!

S: Suddenly everything feels light. I feel nothing anymore.

H: Tell me the date!

S: December 21, 1893.

H: How do you feel now?

S: Good, better than before.

H: If you were to look back, what would you say about this life?

S: It was not pleasant.

H: Did you learn anything?

S: Yes, much.

H: Will you stay where you are now?

S: No, I cannot stay. I still have more to learn.

H: Did you make an important mistake in your last life?

S: Yes.

H: What was it?

S: I should have accepted my husband.

H: Let us go on until something in your present condition changes. What is happening?

S: The pulling—I'm getting a body again.

H: What happens next? When will you be born again?

S: June 12, 1918.

H: You are growing and getting older. Let us go to your tenth year—what is your name now?

S: Varic.

H: Let us proceed further along in your life and stop near the end of it. Where are you?

S: In Cologne and I want to get something to eat. Suddenly there is an air-raid alarm. I'm not familiar with the neighborhood, and I don't know where the air-raid shelters are. The sirens wail —there is a roaring noise—a harsh, roaring noise—a plane—suddenly everything caves in around me—houses collapse—I have to get away from here, I must get away. I run, but I can't run as fast as the others—suddenly everything is so—I'm terribly afraid —and then another house collapses right near me—I feel a sharp pain—a stone hits me in the head—suddenly everything is gone— all gone—I feel like I am floating—I am being released—I am losing shape—I no longer have a body—my body is lying there—I no longer have any connection with this body.

H: But you can see it?

S: Yes—it is underneath the rubble.

H: How do you feel now?

S: Fine.

H: Do you feel any more pain?

S: No.

H: What else do you feel?

S: I have no more feeling for dimensions—everything is very harmonious—I feel very well here—I don't want to return.

H: One life is behind you, right?

S: Yes.

H: Look back for a moment—how was this life?

S: I'm glad it's over. I suffered quite a bit.

H: Did you learn anything?

S: Yes, a great deal.

H: What did you learn above all?

S: To accept myself as I am.

H: Did you make any mistakes?

S: Yes.

H: What kind?

S: I should not have aborted my child.

H: Will you come back into the world again?

S: Yes.

H: Are you glad?

S: No, but it's all right.

H: Let us move forward again until a change takes place. What is happening?

S: I feel the p ll again—I am getting a body.

H: Are you in the womb?

S: Yes.

H: You will be born again soon. When will it be?

S: May 15, 1955.

H: You are being born. You are growing, getting older—we shall go forward in time to the year 1975.

The
End
as the
Beginning

B IRTH AND DEATH are the same. Every ending is also a beginning. May the end of this book be the beginning of new ideas for many. We live in a time of spiritual revolution. Youth is beginning to reorient itself. Satiated with the functional achievements of the Western world, more and more people are turning to spiritual values. The pendulum is swinging in the other direction. Now that the Eastern countries with their spiritual culture have adopted much of the Western thinking and achievements, we in the West are beginning to adopt the wisdom of the East.

It is a great error, however, to believe that the East has a functioning esoteric and that one must therefore study yoga, meditation, I Ching, and Zen. The West has an equally remarkable esoteric tradition. The Western esoteric rests basically on four pillars: astrology, cabala, alchemy, and spiritualism. The Western system is neither better nor worse than the Eastern esoteric, but it was created in our cultural circle and is therefore closer to us in many ways. The time is ripe to take these matters out of the hands of dreamers and visionaries, who in the past did great damage to the reputation of these theories in the eyes of the public.

Starting with this knowledge, we could begin to develop a psychology in the West, because the West as of now still does not possess a true psychology. The only fruitful effort thus far was the analytic psychology of C. G. Jung, but he was probably too far ahead of his time to be understood. Jung recognized clearly what sources one must turn to in order to build a psychology. He studied Eastern teachings, the I Ching, but above all, astrology, alchemy, and Tarot. As of today, he does not seem to have been forgiven this activity.

Man seems to learn best through suffering. Slowly his spiritual suffering has become so pronounced that it has created new opportunities for new thinking. In connection therewith, the idea of reincarnation is a focal point because it opens completely new attitudes toward the world and what goes on in it. Only when man reviews it in its entirety, can he judge and coordinate the details. Development is the task of everyone; our goal is the fully conscious human. In order to become conscious, one must first wake up. Most people are asleep and do not know it. They are machines and day in, day out, they obey their implanted program mechanically and automatically—and at the same time console themselves with the illusion that they are free.

But the individual who is asleep is not aware that he is asleep. He has to wake up first to realize that he was sleeping and that everyone else is sleeping. Gurdjieff, one of the great spiritualists and esoterics of our time, says,

Two hundred aware people, if they existed and considered

it necessary and justifiable, could change all life on earth. But either there are not that many as yet, or they have no desire to do this, or perhaps it is not yet time, or perhaps the other people are all sleeping too soundly.

It is interesting to note how angry people get if it is demonstrated to them that they are only automatons. Hypnosis makes it possible to intervene in a normally functioning program and replace it with another. Thus it is possible to connect various desired actions to the specific signal and to have the suggested action performed posthypnotically, that is, after the hypnosis. If the hypnotized individual is subsequently fully awake, he will answer with the suggested program when the signal is given. For example, one might say, "When I snap my fingers, you will no longer be able to move your arms," or "When I light a cigarette, you will see Santa Claus walking through the room," or "When I give the word, you will embrace everyone here." One is only limited by one's imagination in such experiments.

Such posthypnotic commands are implanted in the subconscious during hypnosis and only brought into play by the signal after the subject is awake again. Here the individual in question will respond to the suggestion completely automatically, even if his behavior is completely unsuitable or illogical. While he is doing it, it is impossible for him to realize that he is doing it. It is a part of him. If one questions him about it and asks him why he is doing it, he will usually try to find a logical-sounding explanation, and he will assure us that he did everything voluntarily. This procedure of attempting to find a subsequent reason for an action that proceeded of its own accord is called "rationalization."

For the audience, such experiments are frequently quite entertaining, but soon some of the observers begin to react aggressively. They begin to discuss the irresponsibility and danger of hypnosis. When a recent German television program presented a show on hypnosis with some of the above-mentioned experiments, the reaction of the public was surprisingly negative.

Without hesitation, everything was labeled a swindle and a fraud. Some emphasized the irresponsibility and the possible dangers. These reactions may be considered a voluntary diversion from the actual message that clearly emanated from this show, namely, that man is a machine and that his programs can be interchanged at will. The normal behavior of an individual, therefore, is in no way different psychologically from that of the hypnotized spectator who, as the result of a posthypnotic command, suddenly performs a belly dance in his waking state.

Such a show is a caricature of human behavior. Those who are caricatured usually react with some anger. But instead of recognizing that man constantly finds himself in a hypnotic-like sleep and obeying the command to finally awaken and become conscious, he prefers to cling to his old illusions and projects his fear outward on hypnosis and the hypnotist. He looks into the mirror and scolds the mirror for what he sees in it. Waking up, however, means, first of all, getting rid of our fixations and thoroughly repolarizing in all areas.

Thorough repolarizing is one of the best, quickest, and safest means of awakening and developing. The law of triangulation provides us with the principle that every opinion, every view, and every judgment we possess is a fixation on one pole of reality. However, reality always encompasses two poles, and only when we have two poles together do we have an entity. As long as a person believes in one specific view, he clings to one pole. For example, I am for A and against B:

+	−
×	×
A	B

To repolarize means to be immediately only for B and against A. If previously we listened only to arguments in favor of A, we now look exclusively for arguments in favor of B and against A. Suddenly point B becomes equal to point A. We can no longer decide which is better and which is right. At this moment something very unusual happens: by recognizing that there are two poles, one is suddenly propelled to a new, third point, C, from which one can now see and comprehend A and B as an entity:

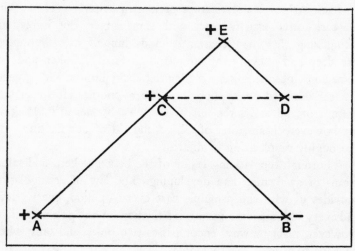

Reaching point C means a step forward in development, which was made possible only by giving up the fixation with point A. The law of polarity, however, immediately provides an antipole for point C, namely, point D. Now we must again go through the same procedure: repolarize at point D in order to be able to reach point E. This principle keeps the learning process flowing and guarantees development. With no great difficulty, we recognize in the law of triangulation the pattern: thesis, antithesis, and synthesis. Unfortunately most of the time we neglect to apply this law to all areas.

We have spoken of life and death and have tried to see both as one entity. To do this, we had to repolarize and discovered

that death is being alive in the hereafter and dead in the present
—life and death are the same; so are being born and dying. Every
end is at the same time a beginning. Every door is at the same
time an entrance and an exit—it simply depends on which side
we are on. And so to end this book, let us look at the beginning
once more . . .

When people learn to recognize all beauty as beauty,
They will begin to recognize ugliness.
When people learn to recognize everything good as
    good,
They will begin to recognize evil.

Therefore:
Existence and nonexistence depend on one another in
    their formation;
The difficult and the easy depend on one another in
    their performance;
Long and short depend on one another in their opposi-
    tion;
High and low depend on one another in their situation;
Front and rear depend on one another in their being
    together.

Therefore, the wise man:
Carries on his business without doing and
Preaches his sermon without words.

All things rise upward, but he does not turn away from
    them;
He gives them life, but does not take possession of them;
He negotiates, but does not appropriate;
He accomplishes, but demands no recognition—
And since he makes no demands on recognition,
Recognition cannot be taken from him.

LAO-TSE

—233

Bibliography

CROWLEY, ALEISTER. *Magic in Theory and Practice*, Krishna Press, 1973.

JUNG, CARL G. *Collected Works*, Princeton University Press, 1954-1972.

LEBOYER, FREDERICK. *Birth Without Violence*, Knopf, 1975.

LINDEN, WILHELM Z. *A Child Is Born*, Anthroposophic Press, 1973.

OUSPENSKY, P. D. *In Search of the Miraculous: Fragments of An Unknown Teaching*, Harcourt Brace Jovanovich, 1965.